TRAILING
GOD

Wisdom for the Soul

KEMI SIJUWADE B. ARCH

WESTBOW
PRESS®
A DIVISION OF THOMAS NELSON
& ZONDERVAN

WestBow Press books may be ordered through booksellers or by contacting:

WestBow Press
A Division of Thomas Nelson & Zondervan
1663 Liberty Drive
Bloomington, IN 47403
www.westbowpress.com
844-714-3454

ISBN: 978-1-6642-2793-4 (sc)
ISBN: 978-1-6642-2794-1 (e)

Print information available on the last page.

WestBow Press rev. date: 04/09/2021

For my loved ones
God is able.

Contents

Preface

I always knew I had something to say about various topics dear to my heart and that I would write about them. But when I heard in my spirit that I needed to write a book to help Christian women worldwide, I thought, *I can't do that*. Although I'm a Christian, I wouldn't consider myself an authority on the Word of God. I am but a flawed woman, after all. Who would want to read anything I wrote? What impact could I possibly make? I promptly dismissed the idea.

In 2019, however, this prompting became stronger, and I knew I could no longer dismiss it. I told myself that before I did any such thing, I had to fully research God and meet with him face-to-face. (Such a lofty proposition!) It had to be a physical revelation of who God is in my life. I had to know that I know. Without him revealing himself to me in such a manner, I could not possibly do this.

So I started a journey of research on who God is. I listened to rabbis, pastors, imams, and priests, as well as to Sadhguru, the Buddha, and the Dalai Lama, trying to find a common thread of God in all their instructions. Still, I did not feel I could see God clearly, so I finally decided to go on an Israel tour. If there was anywhere on earth where I would have this experiential knowledge of God that I so desired, it would be in Israel—to walk on the same grounds that Jesus, the Son of God, had walked.

I made a pact with God that if he was real, I needed him to *prove* he was real in a manner that would be undeniable to me.

In January 2020, I went to Israel with a Christian group. My experience in Israel deserves to be written and shared with all, but even more important was that God met with me in person—quite literally—and showed himself to be real, and I knew I would write this book. I said to God, "Use me, but I am just a scribe. You are the author. I will only write down what you tell me." And it has been that case throughout the writing of this book. God picks the topics, the chapters, and then reveals the Bible verses in an illuminating manner. As I wrote, I was taught by God himself. It has been an exhilarating experience.

Trailing God, the title of this book, also was given by God. I had wanted to title the book *Beauty for Ashes*, but when I received *Trailing God*, I knew I had to research the word *trailing*; it means to drag behind you, to pull something along, to help get something or someone to its final destination. Then, it all made sense to me.

As Christians, we all know what is right. We read our Bibles, we have heard Bible stories, and we strive to be the very best Christian version of ourselves. We struggle, however, through the different circumstances and situations that life throws at us. It is in these instances that we need to know that God sees the frailties of our minds and will help us.

Trailing God is about helping us through these tough life situations. Sometimes, God may have to drag us, kicking and screaming, or literally move us over these hurdles so that we can get to our final destinations—our destinies, our legacies.

This book was started prior to the COVID-19 pandemic in 2020, and as such, some of the topics have touched on the pain and suffering of the people at this time and addressed certain issues.

My prayer is that this book will reach everyone— men, women, aunts, uncles, daughters, sons, presidents, prime ministers, governors, kings and queens—who need comfort and solace and hopefully will answer some of life's nagging questions.

—Kemi

1

The Promises of God, the Principles of God, and the Love of God

———————————————◆————

The Promises of God

The promises of God are his words to us, and those words are *Yea* and *Amen*. This means "yes" and "so be it." He says, "I know the plans I have for you. Plans to prosper you, and not to harm you, plans to give you a future and a hope" (Jeremiah 29:11 NIV). The Lord also says, "I wish above all things that you prosper and be in health, even as your soul prospers" (3 John 2:5 KJV).

These promises show us that God wants only the best for his children. If we hold on to the thought that God wants the best and thinks the best for us, then when those stormy times come in our lives, we can go to his throne of grace and tell him all about it. God will always discuss the situation and provide answers. God answers prayers. How God answers will always be in line with who he is and not who we are. The answer may not reflect what we think or align with what we want, but rest assured, it will be what is best for us. We have to remember that we only see darkly, but God sees everything. He is the Ancient of Days, so he knows the things of the past. He is the "I am that I am," so he knows the present. He is the Alpha and Omega, the beginning and the end, so he knows how it will all end.

How difficult we, his children, find it to trust and surrender. If only we could let his love for us permeate through us.

The promises of God must teach us to trust and surrender. For he has his angels guarding us to prevent us from falling and dashing our feet against a stone (Psalm 91:11–12 NIV).

The Principles of God

Have you ever wondered why the wicked succeed in life? We, God's children, love him, tithe, work hard, and serve, yet we see the children of the wicked succeeding in every area of their lives while we struggle.

It is all about the principles of God. The principles of God are his divine rules that govern both the heavens and the earth.

These principles don't change—not ever. They will always be in operation, once applied. They are like the law of gravity; it is always in effect. The thing about the law of gravity is that it is no respecter of persons. The law of gravity is in effect whether you are a child of God or you worship Satan. So also are the principles of God. They will work, regardless of who you are. If you have inadvertently tapped into them, they still will be in operation. These principles are all over the Bible; you can search for them or ask the Holy Spirit to show you.

An example of God's principles is, "Give and it shall be given on to you, A good measure, pressed down, shaken together and running over shall men give unto your bosom" (Luke 6:38 NKJV).

Giving does not always have to be material things. It could be love, time, emotions—anything, really. If you give your time, learning to play the guitar, eventually, the guitar will give back to you by making you an expert at playing it. It is such a simple principle, but we miss it all the time while we look for a lofty principle of God.

Another example is seed time and harvest time (Genesis 8:22). God says while the earth remains, there will always be seed time and harvest time. Planting time and reaping time. Under this principle also lies the idea that "you will always reap what you sow, God is not mocked" (Galatians 6:8 KJV). This principle of God works for whoever taps into it. If the children of the world tap into this principle and apply it, it will work for them as well. And if a child of God does not realize this principle and does not apply it in his or her life, then the opportunity of using the principle to his or her benefit is lost.

Seed time, in layman's terms, simply means doing what you need to do at the right time so that in the future, when harvest time comes, you can reap from what you have planted.

Here's the thing with this principle: it works with the heart's desire of the person applying it. So if you have evil desires and sow evil seeds, when harvest time comes, you will reap the evil fruits that come up. However, if you sow good seeds, then, when harvest time comes, good fruits will sprout everywhere.

If a mother does not invest in her children when they are young, take them to the Lord, and help them to understand right from wrong, then, when harvest time comes, she will find herself with wayward children who don't know the Lord and who gets into all manners of trouble.

However, since this principle works regardless of who applies it, if a non-Christian understands these principles, it will work in his or her life.

Many principles of God are all over in the Bible, and these principles are always in effect. We, as Christians, need to search the scriptures to find what I call *nuggets* and apply them to our lives so we can have the lives that God intended for us to have. Remember that he has come so that we may have life and life in abundance.

> My people are destroyed for lack of knowledge. (Hosea 4:6 KJV)

The Love of God

> For God so loved the world that he gave his only begotten Son, that whosoever believeth in him should not perish, but has everlasting life.
> —John 3:16 (KJV)

There is no greater love than this. When we say we love, as human beings, most of the time the love is conditional; it is shallow and has no roots. God's love is not as such. If we really think about it, it overwhelms us. It causes us to see the dirty rags with which we cover ourselves—and we proclaim the rags to be love.

God's love is such that nothing can separate us from it. Even when we stray, he still loves us, and he gently brings us back into his loving arms. Love, however, is a two-way thing and works best when there is a relationship involved.

Loving someone who doesn't know who we are is called being a "fan". It is shallow and unresponsive. So also is loving someone who knows who we are but does not love us back—that is unrequited love, which is, for the most part, a painful love. But when we love someone who loves us back, that is wonderful. We want to be with that person all the time. We want to please that person, serve the person, communicate with the person, and share laughter with that person. So also is our God's desire for a relationship with his children. He loves us and wants us to love him back. He wants us to get to know him through the reading of his Word. He wants us to have conversations with him through prayer and listening to him after prayer to hear what he has to say. He wants to have difficult discussions, as well as mundane ones such as, "God, do you know where I left my glasses? Please help me find them"—that's mundane, but he answers such prayers as well. That is communication.

The Bible says, "My sheep know my voice and other voices, they will not follow" (John 10:27 KJV). How do we know his voice? Is it not by training to hear him and constantly listening out for him?

Have you ever wondered about how a newborn baby's eyes follow the mother's voice? How the baby heard the mother's voice while in the womb and recognizes it after he or she is born? The baby, while in the womb, has trained it's ear to listen out for the mother's voice. The baby does not recognize any other voice except the mother's for the first few months of life. The baby only meets the mother after he or she is born but has heard her long before then. That is what it should be like between God and us. We should train ourselves to hear our Father in heaven and recognize his voice so that we may communicate with him and thereby respond to his love.

2

The Proverbs 31 Woman

The Woman of Integrity (Proverbs 31:1–9)

The woman of integrity instructs her son about devious women so that he will not fall into their nets. She says to her son that these women ruin not just ordinary people but kings as well, people of means and stature. Such is their power.

She instructs him on the ills of drinking alcohol to excess. She says to him that excessive drinking is for those who want to forget their problems or their poverty.

This makes you evaluate people when they are nicely dressed, especially at a party, but are only seeking to get drunk. What are they trying to get away from? Is it financial distress? Trouble at home? Business troubles?

What does a woman of integrity do when she comes in contact with such people?

Does she feel pity for them?

Does she join them in drinking?

Does she pray for them when she gets home?

Does she try to stop their drinking at the party?

The woman of integrity instructs her son to speak up for those who are oppressed and cannot speak up for themselves—the destitute, the poor, and the needy. She tells her son always to be on their side and not to cater only to people of means. She urges her son to ensure that the rights of the poor are not trampled on. This he can do through his choice of career and the roles he takes on in his community, or it might just be in helping out disenfranchised people he meets in his daily life. This should be his way of giving back to society.

So Who Is This Woman of Integrity?

A woman of integrity has a noble character. She has fine personal qualities and high moral principles and ideals (Proverbs 31:10).

Her husband trusts her with his life. He has full confidence in her and lacks nothing of value. This means that she provides for him. Her husband is respected by his peers due to the way they perceive him. They can see that he is well looked after (Proverbs 31:11–12, 23).

A woman of integrity is hardworking. She creates and works with eager hands. She is not lazy in any shape or form (Proverbs 31:13, 24).

A woman of integrity looks after her family to ensure that there is food for everyone, including her house servants. No one leaves the house hungry. She cooks for the family and does not leave the feeding of the family to the cook (Proverbs 31:15, 22).

A woman of integrity is also an investor. She buys properties, as a side hustle, from the money she makes from her day job (Proverbs 31:16).

A woman of integrity also has business savvy. She looks after her investments to ensure that they are profitable. She is diligent about tracking her business transactions.

A woman of integrity is very hospitable. She opens her arms to the poor and needy. She helps people (Proverbs 31:20).

A woman of integrity is a wise woman. She speaks wisdom and faithful instructions. She is thoughtful and slow to speak. She searches the truth and speaks from the wisdom that God has granted her. She does not just speak at every turn, without thinking about the situation brought before her. And when she does speak, she speaks from her heart, with faithfulness. She is faithful to both herself and the circumstance when she utters her words of wisdom.

Her husband is very proud of her, and he sings her praises everywhere. He feels very blessed to call her his wife (Proverbs 31:28–29).

Her children observe her as she does all the above. She has modeled before them what a blessed woman is, and so they call her blessed (Proverbs 31:28).

Have we modeled what a blessed woman is to our children, especially our daughters?

Finally, a woman of integrity does all these things because she has a reverential fear of the Lord.

The Bible says, "The fear of the Lord is the beginning of all Wisdom" (Proverbs 9:10 KJV).

Ladies, let us fear the Lord.

3

Bone of My Bone

------◆------

Genesis 2

As mothers, we tend to pray for our sons to find the "bone of my bone, or flesh of my flesh." This means we want them to find a wife that fits them perfectly. However, what does that really mean? Is that the right prayer for our sons?

Where did the above phrase come from?

It came from Adam, the first man, when he first laid eyes on Eve. He called her "woman," as she was formed from the rib that God took from his side (Genesis 2:23).

Since Eve was the "bone of his bone," let's examine who Eve was.

- Eve was gullible. (Genesis 3:2–4).

- Eve was superficial. She looked mainly at the outward appearance (Genesis 3:5).
- Eve was disobedient. She did not listen to the instructions from God (Genesis 3:3).
- Eve did not respect her husband and did not listen to her husband (Genesis 3:6).
- Eve would get her husband into trouble, if it meant getting what she wanted (Genesis 3:6).
- Eve lusted after the apple and therefore listened to Satan (Genesis 3:3–6).
- Eve had pride; she wanted to be like God.

After examining Eve's character, is she really the model wife we want for our sons?

Instead of praying for "bone of my bone" for our sons, we should pray to God that our sons find their own wives—a woman of God, who listens and walks according to God's direction; a woman who submits to her husband. Such a woman has a strong foot in the ways of God and has learned to know God's voice from all other deceitful voices.

This should be our prayer, not bone of our bones.

Let's talk about finding husbands for our daughters—the Adam we are all seeking. But is Adam really the "bone of my bone" for our daughters?

Let's examine Adam, the first man.

Adam was the one to whom God gave the instruction of not eating from the tree of the knowledge of good and evil. God gave Adam this instruction even before Eve was created (Genesis 2:17).

He is the head of the home and the spiritual head of the home. He is the keeper of God's words in his family and the reverence of God's words and instructions.

- Adam, however, did not impress upon Eve the importance of keeping God's words. He was present when Satan presented his ideas to Eve (Genesis 3:6).
- He did not take the lead in his home (Genesis 3:6–7).
- He allowed Eve to make significant *spiritual* decisions for him (Genesis 3:6–7).
- He blamed Eve for the wrong that happened in the home (Genesis 3:17).
- Adam trusted Eve's words more than the words of God (Genesis 3:11).

Think about Adam and his character. Adam was a weak man—not the type of husband we want for our daughters.

So instead of praying for "bone of my bone, or flesh of my flesh" for our daughters, let us pray that God grants her a man who desires to do the will of God; a man who hungers and thirsts after righteousness; a man after God's own heart; a man who loves God above all else and is the spiritual leader of the home.

As mothers, this should be our prayer for our sons and daughters.

4

Ruth

Where you go, I will go and where you
stay, I will stay. Your people will be my
people and your God will be my God.
—Ruth 1:16

The Committed Woman

The above were Ruth's words to Naomi, her mother-in-law. These are the words of a committed woman. Ruth was not only stating her commitment to Naomi but also to Naomi's people and Naomi's God. Ruth was a Moabite woman who chose to leave her pagan gods to join her life with Naomi's and her God.

The question is, what did Ruth see that Orpah failed to see? What brings about such a level of commitment to a God who, according to Naomi, had failed her. Naomi says, "The hand of the Lord is gone out against me" (Ruth 1:13 KJV).

How can Ruth utter such commitment to a God who has allowed all her loved ones to die prematurely? Ruth had witnessed the deaths of her father-in-law, her brother-in-law, and her husband. She must have wondered what kind of God would allow that kind of sorrow to his own people.

Orpah clearly thought the same because the Bible tells us that she decided to go back to her mother's house and her pagan gods (Ruth 1:14).

So again, what did Ruth see?

The Story from Naomi and Ruth's Return to Bethlehem

Naomi gave Ruth permission to glean after the male farmers on Boaz's field (Ruth 2:2),

- Ruth's commitment was seen as she strived to provide food for both herself and Naomi. Isn't it strange that Naomi referred to both Orpah and Ruth as daughters-in-law in Moab, but when Ruth returned with her to Bethlehem, she referred to Ruth as her daughter?

Commitment brings about a change in status, stature, and circumstance.

Ruth found favor with Boaz, the owner of the field, from whom she gathered food.

- Ruth's commitment to Naomi did not go unnoticed by Boaz. In fact, Boaz was so impressed with Ruth that he prayed that Ruth would be richly rewarded by the Lord (Ruth 2:11–12 KJV).

Commitment never goes unnoticed.

Boaz helped Ruth in her endeavor to feed Naomi.

- Boaz made sure that Ruth had more than enough harvested grain to take home by instructing his farmers to leave a lot of barley that she could pick up after them.

Commitment does not go hungry. You will eventually reap from what you have sown.

Naomi chose a husband for Ruth.

- After some time had passed, Naomi decided it was time to find Ruth a loving home of her own, where she would be cared for as Ruth had cared for her. Naomi chose Boaz, who was a kinsman redeemer in her family, for Ruth.

Commitment brings about reciprocity. Naomi was committed to Ruth.

Boaz redeemed.

- Boaz redeemed Naomi's land by buying it from her and thereby inheriting Ruth, the Moabitess, with it. Boaz married Ruth and made her one of the wealthiest women, a noblewoman, of her time. Ruth went from being a woman without a husband, without status, without means, without children, and without God to a woman who had all the above and understood who God is.

Commitment brings about redemption.

So what did Ruth see?

Ruth saw her redemption through Naomi. And through Naomi, she inadvertently saw God.

Ladies, let us ask the Lord to help us see his redemptive power at work in our lives and in the lives of our loved ones, family, and friends.

5

Esther

The Obedient Woman

The story of Esther is that of an obedient woman who, through her obedience to God; to Mordecai - her uncle; to Hegai - king's eunuch in charge of the harem; and to King Xerxes was able to save her people from imminent death.

But before we look at Esther, let's look at another woman in this story—Queen Vashti, who was a direct contrast to Esther.

Queen Vashti

Queen Vashti was an incredibly beautiful woman. She was so beautiful that her husband, the king, wanted to show off her beauty to his nobles and officials. Queen Vashti was very vain, and she put her beauty before respecting her husband. And through disrespecting her husband, the king, she unleashed marital issues and problems in the homes of the people living in that region.

Queen Vashti was later deposed by the king, and her reign as the queen ended. Another woman, a virgin, was to be made queen instead. Queen Vashti's deposition was made public, and huge was the disgrace. What she had intended to do to the king—publicly humiliating him and disgracing him among his underlings—was exactly what happened to her.

Ladies, be careful to hold your husbands with high esteem, both privately and publicly. Always respect him, whether he has money or not. God has placed him over you for a reason.

My prayer is that we, as wives, will not be publicly disgraced or humiliated.

Now, let's look at the obedience of Esther and the results of her obedience.

Esther

Esther was beautiful, but she did not let it go to her head. Instead, when she arrived at King Xerxes's harem, of which Hegai, the eunuch, was in charge, Esther found favor with Hegai (Esther 2:9). The result of pleasing the eunuch was extra-special beauty treatments and the best living conditions for her.

Moral: Ladies, be nice to people you come across. You never know who has the key to your elevation.

Esther listened to her elders. She did not pretend to know everything or the ways of the world. So when Mordecai, her uncle, told her not to mention her nationality or family background, she obeyed without hesitation (Esther 2:10).

Moral: Mothers, let's teach our children to listen to instruction from their elders. Let's train our kids to be respectful of elders and to learn from their own experiences of life.

Esther was also very humble and full of humility (Esther 2:15–16). She listened to Hegai's instructions, and when it was her turn to visit King Xerxes, she took with her only the items that Hegai had given her. She found favor with all the people she came across.

Moral: Humility attracts favor—favor from God as well as others. Let us learn to be humble.

Esther found favor with King Xerxes, and he made Esther his queen.

Moral: When you have God's favor, he will take you from a lowly place and set you up high in places that others can only dream of. Promotion comes from God (Psalm 75:6).

Esther learned from Mordecai about the king's decree to kill the Jews—remember that Esther had not disclosed to anyone that she was a Jew—and this was distressing news to her (Esther 4:4).

Moral: Be compassionate. When God has lifted you to high places, don't forget the ones you left behind, especially when they are in trouble.

Esther chose to help her people, rather than be queen. She knew of the king's decree that stated she could see him only if he summoned her, but the issue at hand was more important to her, so she chose to go see him without his invitation, thereby risking her life for her people. The punishment for those who displeased the king generally was death (Esther 4:9), but Esther did not carry out this without first fasting and praying to God. She asked all the Jews to pray for three days before she went in front of the king. She sought the Lord (Esther 4:15).

Moral: It is good to be brave when we're in a terrible situation, but braveness alone is not enough. We need to seek the Lord's face before taking any steps to rectify a situation. Do not go it alone without God on your side.

> If God be for us, who can be against us.
> (Romans 8:31 KJV)

Esther was a wise woman. She knew that the way to a man's heart was through his stomach, and if a man was pleased with his meal, she could ask him anything and most likely get a favorable answer. She also knew that she shouldn't approach her husband with a problem without ensuring that he was happy with her first. So Queen Esther invited King Xerxes and Haman, the perpetrator of evil against the Jews, to a banquet.

Moral: Study your husband. Find out what makes him happy—King Xerxes liked banquets and a good party—and do that first, before approaching him with a problem or a wish. It might be a certain food, his family, or sex. Give him what he wants first; then he will give you what you want. So it is too with God.

> Seek first the kingdom of God and its Righteousness and all these things shall be added on to you. (Matthew 6:33 ESV)

> Delight yourself in the Lord and he will grant you the desires of your heart. (Psalm 37:4 NKJV)

Esther told the king of Haman's plot to kill her people, and she asked that her people be spared. Haman and his family were hanged, and the Jews were freed from the edict to have them killed on a certain date, which had gone out to all provinces.

Moral: Because of Esther's obedience, bravery, and wisdom to know that God is above all things and all situations, God elevated her to a position of influence, and she was able to set her people free from imminent death.

Sometimes, God puts you in high places, not for yourself but for others, that you might be the help in time of need for people who may have no other options.

Let us be sensitive to the call of God in our lives. Let's seek him always to see why he has placed us where he has us:

- As a mother
- As a wife
- As a friend
- As a family member
- As a CEO of a company
- As a church leader or choir leader
- As a committee leader
- As a pastor
- As a boss

Whatever position we find ourselves in, let us always ask God, "Why am I here?"

6

When You Make the Lord Your Shepherd

Psalm 23

In life, we are constantly on the move because life demands it. We have to go to work and deal with issues there; we have to look after the home, pay bills, look after the children, and attend to their needs and the needs of our husbands. We have to give our time to family and friends. We are constantly on the move because we're afraid of being left behind.

Our Lord understands this and wants us to make him our shepherd. If he is our shepherd, then he leads us, guides us, protects us, and—when we stray—comes in search of us. He also wants to provide for us.

But we want to go it alone, thinking we can manage without him. The result of this running around culminates in stress, illness, a frazzled heart, discontentment, and tiredness of the soul.

> The Lord is my Shepherd, I shall not want. (Psalm 23:1 KJV)

First Promise

Here's the first promise: we will not lack if we make him our shepherd. He looks after our needs. The Lord also understands our need to stop and smell the roses— and I mean the Lord understands this quite literally, as in the next few verses, the Lord speaks of green pastures, still waters, and restoration of the soul. The Lord wants to restore us after we've gone through the rigors of life. He says, *Dare to make me your shepherd, and I will bring about peace in your life—a quietness in your soul that only I, the Lord, can give.*

Second Promise

Once you have attained his peace, and he guides you in his righteous ways, his next promise is that of protection.

> Yea, though I walk through the valley of
> shadow of death, I will fear no evil for
> thou art with me, thy rod and thy staff,
> they comfort me. (Psalm 23:5 KJV)

God does not want any evil to harm to you. He wants you to know that he is always present with you, even when you don't feel him there. Even when you feel your world is slowly coming apart at the seams, he is there. The level of protection he assures you is a guarantee of his angels guarding and lifting you up when you fall or are about to dash your foot against a stone (Psalm 91:10). Such is the protection of our God.

Third Promise

His next promise to you is to show you off to your enemies. He is very proud of who you have become by allowing him to be your shepherd. The Bible says he sets a table before you in the presence of your enemies. Setting a table is what you do when you have a special guest in your home. You bring out your best crockery and serve the best meal. This is how our Lord sees us and values us when we make him our shepherd. God wants your enemies to see that he is looking after you and providing for you in a highly esteemed manner. In this same way, he was so proud of Job that he introduced Job to Satan, saying, "Have you considered my son Job?" Job had made the Lord his shepherd, and God was proud of him.

Fourth Promise

God also anoints your head with oil, and your cup runs over. When the Lord anoints you, he sets you apart as his chosen one and then ensures that your cup runs over. This means that you have everything you want and then some. When your cup runs over, it spills down your generational line, and the impact is felt to the third and fourth generations. This is called a generational blessing, which comes only from God.

Fifth Promise

The final promise is the greatest promise of all.

> Surely goodness and mercy shall follow you all the days of your life and you shall dwell in the house of the Lord for ever and ever. (Psalm 23:6 KJV)

This promise is a certainty, a promise of God's goodness and God's mercy—two of God's attributes that we cannot do without. To know that the Lord will always have mercy, regardless of how badly we behave, and that his goodness will always be attainable and within reach—what could be greater than that?

We also know that we get to live with him in his house—the Lord's house—and sit at his footstool and gaze upon his holiness.

These are all the promises we have, if we make the Lord our shepherd.

- We receive God's peace.
- We receive God's protection.
- We receive God's presence in darkness.
- God shows us off to our enemies.
- We don't lack any good things.
- We receive God's abundant provision.
- Our children's children get these abundant provisions as well.
- We receive God's goodness and mercy.
- We get to live with God.

I would say that we can never go wrong with making the Lord our shepherd.

7

Beauty for Ashes

---◆---

Isaiah 61

I discovered Isaiah 61 today for the first time in my life. Although I have always known of the phrase "beauty for ashes," I discovered today that God already had a plan for the "heaviness of our soul."

Not only does he have a plan, but he also has blessings, in order to uproot us from the depths of mourning into which our hearts tend to sink in times of crisis.

As women, God created us differently from men. He created us to be nurturers, givers, helpmates, and lovers. These areas perfectly merge with a man's psyche.

> For this reason, a man would leave his
> father and mother and cleave unto his
> wife and the two shall become one flesh.
> (Genesis 2:24 KJV)

We are created to complement the man, but because of how we are created and the purpose of our creation, God made us highly emotional beings. We tend to feel things deeply—joy, sadness, happiness, depression. It doesn't matter what the emotion is; when it hits us, it hits us hard.

A man's pain is different. It is always temporary, and after a while, he will separate himself from the pain and move on. Case in point: when David's son— the first son he had with Bathsheba (Uriah's wife)— was sick and dying, David fasted for days with ashes on his head, pleading with God to save his son from death. But when he eventually learned that his son had died, David got up, had a bath and a change of clothing, and went to eat. His time of pain was over; he had done what he could and was now moving on. So it is with a man, but I'm sure it was not as easy for Bathsheba to move on so quickly after the loss of her son.

Man was not created with this intensity of emotion. He is a hunter and a gatherer. This is why, in a divorce, a man may be in pain for a little while, but after a time, he will be married to another woman and have kids.

This is how he is created. Even God says, "It is not good for a man to be alone." That which a woman brings into his life is missing, and so he hunts for another to fill that role.

The woman in a divorce, however, cannot move on quite as easily. She suffers from the pain and sorrow that come from the death of a marriage; in some cases, she never remarries.

Yes, I understand this impasse—it's like a cage over our hearts; nothing is allowed in or out. We are at a standstill, unable to move forward, unable to think straight, unable to make future plans, unable to praise God for what we have left, and unable to see God—but *God sees us*.

God understands these states, and even before we go through them, he already has made provision to get us out of them.

> To appoint unto them that mourn in Zion, to give unto them beauty for ashes, the oil of joy for mourning, the garment of praise for the spirit of despair, that they might be called the

trees of righteousness, the planting of
the Lord, that he might be glorified.
(Isaiah 61:3 KJV)

The truth is that God has a plan, and his plan is to
make use of our pain, if we allow him. If we choose
not to allow him to do so, then we, quite literally, will
die in our pain, for the heart can only take so much
sorrow.

Hope deferred makes the heart sick.
(Proverbs 13 KJV)

In the dark periods of our lives, we need to turn
to God. He has allowed us to go through this pain
and sorrow for a reason. And the ultimate reason is
to glorify him. It does not seem that way in times of
trouble, and the *why* questions flood our minds. But
if we turn to him and surrender the pain to him, he
has promised the following:

- Beauty for ashes
- Oil of joy for mourning
- Garment of praise for spirit of heaviness
- Trees of righteousness

What Does "Beauty for Ashes" Mean?

For the most part, what men call beauty is the outward appearance of a man or woman—what a man or woman looks like. When the prophet Samuel was told to anoint the next king of Israel from the household of Jesse, he looked at the outward appearance of Jesse's sons. He kept thinking, with one after the other, *It's this one*, because of his looks. God had to keep telling him, *No, not this one. No, not this one either*, until he led Samuel to David.

> Man looks at the outward appearance,
> but God looks at the heart. (1 Samuel
> 16:7 NKJV)

The beauty spoken of here is not physical beauty. The physical beauty? That is the ashes—the ashes of our lives; those things that belong to the earth that the earth claims back. Remember that we are only clay, an earthen vessel. We will leave the things that we find on earth when we depart the earth—those things are the ashes.

The Bible speaks of these ashes:

> Lay not up for yourselves treasures upon
> earth, where moth and rust doth corrupt

and where thieves break through and steal. (Matthew 6:19 KJV)

God wants to replace those things with beauty—his beauty, the beauty of the heart and spirit—a spirit that relates to God and puts him first in all things and a heart that bears witness to him. That is true beauty.

This beauty transforms us from within, and the effects are seen on the outside. That is when people see us and say to themselves, "Hmm, there is something about that woman," although they can't pinpoint what it is.

The Oil of Joy for Mourning

Psalm 23 says, "He anoints our head with oil and our cup runs over" (KJV).

When the Lord gives us oil of joy for our mourning, he is telling us that this sorrow and sadness will not overwhelm our lives. The mourning will be for a short while. As he pours the oil of joy on us, we begin to experience joy again. It may not be while we are in the middle of the crisis, but as time goes by, the pain lessens, and we begin to see God's hands and provision in our lives. He was there all along, even during the crisis, but our eyes were clouded with pain, making it difficult to see him. Once the oil of joy starts to pour, however, our cups run over, and all we can do is praise him in the midst of the healing of our hearts.

Garment of Praise for Spirit of Heaviness

Pain endures for a while, but joy comes in the morning. As the daughters of the Most High, the King, we must learn to find God in the midst of our crises. For when we see God, we will see his attributes, which, in turn, causes us to praise him. He offers us the garment of praise. Our Bible says that God inhabits the praises of his people (Psalm 22:3). God is a miracle-working God and a way-maker. So if we praise him and know that he dwells in our praises, we are inherently having a meeting with God and petitioning him regarding our circumstances. This is why when it becomes difficult to pray, we must endeavor to praise him, even in the midst of pain.

God sees our hearts and our pain; we do not need to tell him anything. He is the one who heals us, right in the middle of our praise and worship of him. In praise and worship, we surrender all to him and give him full access to use our pain to bring glory to himself. In so doing, God makes us his trees of righteousness. He does the planting himself, making us deeply rooted in him.

How Do We Become Trees of His Righteousness?

As trees of righteousness, we seek to do God's will. We represent God here on earth. Our pain no longer engulfs us, for we have learned from it. And we have seen God in the midst of it. As trees of righteousness, we now seek to help others who are going through similar circumstances and take them to God in prayer. By doing so, we are sharing the love of God with people who may not necessarily know him, thereby drawing others to him.

Consider Joyce Meyer, the TV evangelist, for example. Joyce went through a traumatic time as she was growing up; her father repeatedly sexually abused her. God worked through her pain, and though it took many years (pain had formed deep roots in her), she eventually was completely healed and forgave her father. Now, she helps others who silently are going through the same experience; she lets them know that God can heal them too, if they surrender everything—pain and all—to him.

He will use our pain to bring glory to his name. Joyce Meyer has brought millions of people to the

Lord. That is what God means when he says he has planted us to be his trees of righteousness.

You may ask, "What's in it for me, for all the pain I've suffered?"

Remember that God is a just God. He is also a faithful God. He will not let you suffer for nothing. He promises the following:

- We will become his builders—builders of his kingdom, builders of generations, builders of the people of God (Isaiah 61:4).
- We will have helpers and support staff in our businesses and in our lives. Those will come into our lives specifically to help us realize our dreams (Isaiah 61:5).
- We shall be called priests of God, and people shall call us ministers of God (Isaiah 61:6).
- We shall eat the riches of the Gentiles (Isaiah 61:5). Men shall pour into our bosoms all manners of blessings (Isaiah 61:6).
- For all the shame and suffering we have endured, we shall have double portions of blessings for it. "Double for your trouble" (Isaiah 61:7 KJV).
- Our children will be known for good around the world and among the people. People around

them will acknowledge them as being blessed by the Lord (Isaiah 61:8).

Let us be humble, even in the midst of our pain, and surrender it all to God, for he is the beginning and the end—The Alpha and Omega.

8

Your Finances

Money answereth all things.
—Ecclesiastes 10:19

Who Is Money?

Is money a person? No, but money has a persona. The persona of money is seen through the owner.

If the owner of money is generous, then money goes out to be a blessing to others. But if the owner is evil, then money goes out to be an instrument of evil.

The persona of money is that of a servant who needs to be sent out on errands. Money does not like to be in situ—to stay in one place without purpose. It likes direction. Money would yield itself to anyone in search of it. It's not concerned about how you find it but that you send it in a particular direction.

For example, a philanthropist uses his money to build a sick kids hospital where the less privileged can take their kids. In this case, money has been sent in the direction of help.

Another example: a man uses his own money to buy guns for the sole purpose of murder or armed robbery. Money does not say to its owner, *No, I am not going. Your purpose is evil.* It does precisely what its owner wants. In this case, money has been sent in the direction of evil.

Money is not loyal to good or bad deeds. It is loyal to being sent.

The one thing, however, that the money persona does not do well is being kept for no purpose at all; for example, people with lots of it who don't know what to do with it. ("Money miss road" is what we call these people where I come from.) If you check in a few years with such people, you will find that, somehow, they have squandered it away. Such is the case with many lottery winners. They came into money but had no purpose for it. Therefore, money left them. Money needs purpose. Money needs action. It needs to fulfill a purpose in the life of its owner.

Money helps to achieve dreams and to acquire

comfort. It is a helper, and the Bible says it *answereth all things*. Money demands respect. How you use it and what knowledge and wisdom is applied when using it matters to money. Money wants to know if the owner has a concept of who it is and how to apply it.

In the hands of someone with great understanding and wisdom (e.g., Oprah Winfrey), a small amount of money can be turned into billions because that person has learned the concept of who money is. But in the hands of the unlearned, money quickly disappears.

A fool and his money are soon parted.
(Proverbs 21:20 KJV)

Money can afford us comfort, which is not necessarily a bad thing, but money is not meant to be loved. Money is in our lives to serve. The minute we begin to fall in love with it, money turns on us and changes our personas.

For the love of money is the root of all evil. (1 Timothy 6:10 KJV)

Once we fall in love with money, it turns inward to us and not outward to serve. Instead of being a servant, it becomes a conduit for transformation—and this transformation is never for good.

- We become pompous.
- We disregard and disrespect money and people.
- We think of ourselves only and what we want.
- We become boastful.
- We don't care for others who are less privileged.
- We don't send money out for good anymore.
- We are never satisfied with how much of it we have. We always want more.

If we persist in this love of money, it eventually destroys us and invariably leaves.

> No one can serve two masters. Either he will hate one and love the other, or he will be devoted to one and despise the other. You cannot serve both God and money. (Matthew 6:24 KJV)

God knows that the love of money can turn us, and that is why he protects us by telling us to tithe the first 10 percent of our income. He does this for our sake, not for his. He is the Creator God; he can create as much money as he needs for his purpose. He does not need our money to fulfil his purpose. However, he does not want our love for him to be tainted with the love of money.

If you are able to give the first 10 percent of your income to him, then you will know that the love of money does not have a hold over you. But if you have an issue with parting with your 10 percent or even being a giver, then the love of money is taking root in your heart—and the end thereof is ruin.

Satan knows this as well. It's his way of preventing you from doing God's will. Remember that Satan is always at odds with God in every way. So if he can get you to disobey God's words or principles (as he did in the garden of Eden), then he wins.

The first thing Satan will tell you when it comes to tithing is that If you give the first 10 percent of your income, how will the remaining 90 percent ever be enough to cover your needs? The next thing you know, you will cut the amount back or not give at all.

The truth is that when you put that 10 percent down, you will have released yourself from the stronghold of the devil.

> Submit yourself to God, Resist the devil and he will flee from you. (James 4:7 KJV)

Then watch how God meets all your needs and then some. He has promised that eyes have not seen, ears have not heard, neither has come into the heart of man the things that he has for those who love him and are called according to his purpose" (1 Corinthians 2:9 KJV).

Do you love God more than money? Then the above promise is for you.

As mothers and daughters of the Most High God, let's understand who money is. Send it on profitable errands. Keep money doing the good work of God, and be sure to let him know that you are in control of it, not the other way around.

9

Where Sin Abounds

Grace abounds even more.
—Romans 5:20

In the last few weeks, I have been dealing with an experience that has made me see evil face-to-face. It has made me evaluate the words of the Bible verse, "When sin abounds, grace abounds even more."

I found that I was about to become the next victim of cyber fraud and theft. One day, I got a call at seven o'clock in the morning from fraudsters who pretended to be my bank agents, telling me that my credit card had been compromised. I am sure many of us have gotten these crank calls and promptly dismissed the fraudsters, but that morning, they caught me in a state of fear, as I was worried that my son might be stuck in a snowbank or something—it had been snowing heavily over the past few days—and it was way too early in the morning for me to get a regular call.

In my state of anxiety, it was very easy for them to get me hooked on the lies they were feeding me. Of course, I did all they asked, including giving them access into my computer, ostensibly so they could show me how much they claimed had been taken from my credit card and account. This was all in an effort to convince me that they were legitimate but actually was to get access to my personal information and online banking details.

They kept me on the phone for about an hour, perpetuating this hoax. I spoke with three individuals who pretended to work in three different departments of the bank, including the fraud department, no less.

It took me a little while to catch on, but when they asked me to use my credit card to commit fraud, as part of their investigative process, I flat-out refused. I told them I needed that instruction to come directly from the fraud investigations officer, written out on paper with the bank letterhead and signed with authorization from him.

As soon as they realized I wouldn't cooperate, they dropped the call—and that's when it dawned on me that they were con artists. I immediately called my bank and made them check my accounts to ensure no money had been stolen. My account seemed normal; no unusual activity had taken place in the last hour, I was told.

I thought I had escaped being defrauded—a narrow escape, I thought. A week later, I found out that $5,700 had been taken from my accounts for "pseudo" legitimate payments to the Canadian Revenue Agency (CRA) and 407 toll fees.This has led to weeks of trying to recover the money from these institutions.

Why did I tell you about this experience? I'm not the first to experience such a situation, and neither will I be the last. The story, however, does not end there.

It's this next part of the story that makes me think of the Bible phrase, "The heart of man is deceitful above all things and desperately wicked, who can know it?" (Jeremiah 17:9 KJV).

During the course of my bank's investigation, the fraud investigation officer looked into my accounts and insisted that the disputed withdrawals from my accounts were legitimate, as I had made the payments directly to the CRA and 407. I was totally stunned, as I had done no such thing—and I told him so. Eventually, I relayed the entire story of what had happened. After he listened intently, he said he thought he knew what had happened:

So what happened you ask? Here's the kicker. Wait for it.........

Because I refused to commit a crime for the fraudsters with my credit card, and so the end result of their scam, after they had spent over an hour talking to me, was nothing for them, they then proceeded to take money from my accounts and pay everyone to whom I had made a payment to at one time or the other. They distributed my money like I was Santa Claus. Because they weren't successful with their scam, they decided to make me suffer by trying to retrieve my money from the various institutions to which they sent it. I had wasted their time, so they were going to waste mine.

The thought of this made me feel sick. I saw how desperately wicked the heart of man had become and the depths to which it had sunk. It wasn't enough that they were common thieves; but the mere hatred of complete strangers, just because they were unsuccessful with their scam, now, that is evil.

What turns men's hearts so against their fellow human being, who is a complete stranger to them? Someone who has no connection to them, and they don't know what he or she was going through in their world?

How have we become so callous that we do not care what we do to one another? How have we become so desperate in the current world and sunk so low as to blatantly ask another person to commit fraud? We are no longer picking pockets without the knowledge of the victim, but now we confront innocent people and tell them to give you access to their accounts so we can steal from them.

When Jesus says that there are only two commandments we are to obey, and all other laws fall under these two laws. We might think, *Just two laws? That's easy for people to follow*—but that's not true.

Law 1: "Love the Lord with all your heart, mind, and soul" (Matthew 22:37 NIV).

Law2: "Love your neighbor as yourself" (Matthew 22:39 NIV).

Two laws. How difficult can these be to follow? But here I am experiencing what happens when those laws do not influence the decisions that we make.

My heart breaks about this. No, I have not lost money—I will eventually retrieve the money that was sent out—but my heart breaks for the heart of humankind and the slow descent into the pits of hell, where humankind's heart seems to be heading. But

God says, "Where sin abounds, grace abounds even more."

If grace abounds even more, what does that look like? The Bible says the grace of God brings about salvation. God is compassionate and gracious and desires that all individuals receive his salvation.

I know that as wicked as the heart of humankind is, God has already made a provision of redemption to claw us back from the edges of the pit of hell. This is what God's grace is.

With this knowledge, my spirit is lifted, knowing that even for these fraudsters, God has a salvation plan. All I can do right now is pray that laborers are sent on their paths to tell them of God's love and salvation plan, so that those two laws become meaningful in their lives.

Darkness will never overcome light, for God's light will shine into their world of darkness, and though their darkness won't comprehend it, *change shall surely come.*

10

The Temple of God

The Sexual Immorality Sin
1 Corinthians 6:19

The Bible tells us that our bodies are temples of the Holy Spirit (1 Corinthians 6:19). In order to have the Holy Spirit living in us, we need to first commit ourselves to God, receive his salvation, and accept Jesus Christ as our Lord and Savior. Then we can ask the Holy Spirit to reside in us.

If you have never done that, then I urge you to do so quickly. Nothing else is more important than committing yourself to the Lord.

For those of us who have been born again and the Holy Spirit is residing in us, then this is for us.

A woman's body has been used for many things.

This is a beautiful thing that God has given us to house his Spirit and to bring pleasure to our husbands. But it also has been used as power to attain wealth or for sexual gratification to overcome a deeper problem or need in our lives. It has been used to seduce men as a way of controlling them. It has been used as weapons in the marital home to ensure that we got our way. It has been used to destroy other marriages and used for many more illicit acts.

However, the Bible tells us a secret, another hidden nugget. Bodies house not just the Holy Spirit but our spirits as well. The sexual act, though very pleasurable, also has a spiritual aspect to it. The very act is an intermingling of spirits. The Bible says, "He who unites himself with a prostitute is one with her in body" (1 Corinthians 6:16 NIV). The two shall become one.

Guess what, ladies? When we bed-hop in the interest of power or wealth, jumping in and out of sexual relationships with this highly seductive weapon we have, we are totally diluting our own spirits with the spirits of the men we sleep with. Who knows what spirits inhabit those men? By so doing, we open our spirits to accept theirs, and vice versa. If they have evil spirits in them, we inadvertently open ourselves up to their evil spirits. Multiply that by the number of sexual relationships we have had in our lives, yet we wonder why things are so difficult or why our prayers take so long before we see answers.

God answered our prayers the minute we prayed. Please don't get that wrong. But the time line of receiving those answered prayers is the battle that takes place between God's angels who bring the answers to us and the forces of darkness that we have allowed in through sex.

The Bible says, "Flee from sexual immorality. All other sins a man commits are outside of his body, but he who sins sexually, sin against his own body" (1 Corinthians 6:18 NKJV).

Outside of the evil that we inadvertently may have allowed to reside in our spirits, how about the sin against the body itself; the sexual disease that is transmitted in the process of bed-hopping; sins such as AIDS, venereal disease, syphilis, gonorrhea, and many more? These diseases are transmitted because we do not revere God with body, mind, and soul.

A sexual sin does not just destroy one aspect of life; it destroys three: the body, the mind, and the soul.

The body—sexual diseases

The soul—allowing familiar spirits into yours through sex

But let's talk about the destruction of the mind. How will your mind be destroyed?

When you cheat on your husband, it calls for lying; your mind is destroyed.

When you have multiple partners, it calls for lack of peace, as you are trying to ensure that no one finds out about the other; your mind is destroyed.

When you have sexual partners over the years, it calls for comparison of one man to another, and you are never satisfied sexually with your current partner; your mind is destroyed.

When you have several partners, you reduce God's special pleasurable act between a husband and wife to just an animalistic act that brings no spiritual or emotional connection between the parties involved; your mind is destroyed.

That is how the mind gets destroyed. In the end, did we acquire wealth or power? Did we get our way in the home? Did we control the men? The answer likely is yes to all those questions but at what cost? And was it worth it in the end?

But here's the most important fact that the Bible emphasizes: "Do you know that your bodies are members of Christ himself" (1 Corinthians 6:15 KJV).

How can we say we love and revere God and then

take his members and unite them with every Tom, Dick, and Harry who says sweet nothings in our ears?

Ladies, our love of God must occupy the highest position in our lives, even our sex lives. This way, we will show the world that we are the daughters of the Most High God.

11

The Tongue - Power of Life and Death

Proverbs 18:21

The tongue is a powerful instrument in our bodies. I have always known that we can use our tongues to uplift or to bring down. The Bible says that the power of life and death is in the tongue (Proverbs 18:21).

But what do we really know about the tongue? Do we know how powerful it is? Do we know what else the Bible says about the tongue? And when we do know what the Bible says, how are we to use it?

I have always wondered how we can bring someone completely down, destroying another human being with our tongues, to the extent that the person sometimes considers suicide.

Yet with this same tongue, we can uplift another soul and bring joy and happiness into someone's life.

We say that words are just words, but those words are formed by the tongue. If we don't have tongues, we can't speak. Even when we have thoughts in our minds, good or bad, we are not able to express them in words to another human being without the tongue.

I'm certain most of us understand this, as I do. What we really need to consider is how something as tiny as the tongue has such powerful synergy with reality.

My journey to research the tongue in the Bible took me to James 3:5, which states:

> The tongue also is a fire, a world of evil among the parts of the body. It corrupts the whole person, sets the whole course of his life, and it is itself set on fire by hell. (KJV)

In reading the above, I see that the tongue, without God, is completely evil. It does not edify in any manner, and it corrupts the person. You might say that you're a nice person and speak nice things about people, so how can your tongue be evil?

The Bible says that out of the abundance of the heart, the mouth speaks (Matthew 12:34).

A heart without God is evil all the times (Jeremiah 17:9–11). The heart is deceitful above all things and desperately wicked. Who can know it?

When you put those two verses together, you will understand that a heart that does not have Jesus Christ at its center will always have deceitful and wicked thoughts. These thoughts could be toward another human being or toward oneself. Eventually, these thoughts come out in words that are powerful. The words embody the wicked thoughts so that they completely destroy the person at whom the words are directed.

The Bible says, "No man can tame the tongue, it is a restless evil, full of deadly poison" (James 3:8 KJV).

Yes, no man can tame the tongue, but the Holy Spirit helps us in this regard. When we make Jesus Christ our Lord and Savior, he sends us his Holy Spirit who now lives in us and helps us in the renewing of our minds, so that we may now speak words of edification and life into others and ourselves.

Below are a few verses from the Bible that speak about the menace our words can create in our lives and the lives of others. Proverbs 18 devotes several passages to our words to ensure that we get this.

A fool finds no pleasure in understanding
but delights in airing his own opinions.
(Proverbs 18:2 KJV)

Take time to listen to others in order to understand where they are coming from before airing your own opinion. Do not be quick to judge a situation without listening first; you may learn something you never considered.

The words of a man's mouth are deep
waters. (Proverbs 18:4 KJV)

Have you ever gone deep-sea diving? The sea *is* deep, isn't it? So are the words that we utter. They go down deep into the soul. We need to be careful not to break the spirit of the recipient with our words. As mothers, we should be extremely mindful of this when speaking to our children, or as wives when speaking to our husbands.

A fool's lips bring him strife. (Proverbs
18:6 KJV)

What words do you say to yourself? Have you inadvertently brought strife into your own life by your words? You can either speak life into your spirit, or you can speak death. The choice is yours. God has given you free will.

> A fool's mouth is his own undoing and his lips are a snare to his soul. (Proverbs 18:7 KJV)

A snare is a trap. You can trap yourself in an unfavorable situation by the words of your mouth, and in so doing, it can become your undoing.

Knowing all that is written in the Bible regarding the tongue, what do we do with it, as mothers, aunts, and daughters of the Most High? We use it to speak life and for edification in our lives and the lives of others. We must be slow to speak, and when we do speak, we try to do so without anger, frustration, or strife. Whatever we speak becomes our reality or the reality of others.

> The power of life and death is in the tongue.
> —Proverbs 18:21

12

Entrapment

And the Lord's servant must not quarrel, instead he must be kind to everyone, able to teach, not resentful. those who oppose him, he must gently instruct, in the hope that God will grant them repentance leading them to knowledge of the truth. And they will come to their senses and escape from the trap of the devil, who has taken them captive to do his will.

—2 Timothy 2:24–26 (KJV)

Entrapment is an action of tricking someone into committing a crime in order to secure that person's prosecution.

In life, you may take offense to something that someone did or said or how the person behaved toward you. As human beings, we are upset when this happens. We want to prove our point to the perpetrator of the offense, or sometimes, we tell others about the offense and want them to see things from our perspective.

We don't look beyond what is in front of us. All we see is the offense and the perpetrator. This is a fight we think we must win. We want an apology, and if we don't get one, then we want to cast the person out of our circle of friends. But what happens when we stop focusing on the physical— the offense, the person—and look at this from a spiritual perspective?

The Bible tells us that the thief has come to steal, kill, and destroy (John 10:29). You might ask what does "steal, kill, and destroy" have to do with two friends quarreling? Well, a lot! When you quarrel with a friend, and it can't be resolved with kindness and a teachable moment but ends up in strife, then the devil has stolen, the devil has killed, and the devil has destroyed.

The years of friendship prior to the quarrel have been stolen from both parties. The current friendship has been killed and destroyed. Some friendships are never repaired, and households sometimes become lifelong enemies.

But God tells us to be as wise as serpents and not always take what is going on at face value, even when it is so obvious that the person with whom you are quarreling is wrong.

As daughters of the Most High, let's be cognizant of the devil's entrapment of others; he is always looking for humans to do his bidding. The devil roams around, seeking someone to devour.

No one is without sin, and no one is right all the time, except God. When we find ourselves in these situations, let's be gentle in our conversations and not be resentful but admonish the other person with love, gently bringing him or her around to our point. By doing so, we will lead him or her out of the devil's entrapment.

And if we are not successful at doing this with others, let's hope that they will come to their senses and be able to escape the entrapment of the devil on their own. Let's also pray for them in this regard.

We should also examine ourselves and search our own motives for wanting our thoughts or decisions to be the predominant thought in our discussions. We need to ensure that our thoughts and motives are pure; otherwise, there is work to be done on both sides. As daughters of the Most High God, let us elevate our relationships in love, kindness, and thoughtfulness, with wisdom from above, that we may encourage one another, build up one another, and not allow ourselves to be entrapped by the devil.

13

Wives and Husbands

---

1 Peter 3:1–7; Ephesians 5:22

The topic of this chapter is husbands and wives—
marriage. I am not qualified to write on this topic
because I am currently divorced, with a son, but when
I was married, it lasted only three years before we
separated and eventually divorced. I am a student
here as well, learning the topic as the Lord uses me to
impart his deep mysteries of marriage to us all.

So let's dissect what happened in my marriage,
why it failed on my part. I will admit I interpreted
the word *submission* badly. I thought submission was
saying sorry all the time and losing oneself completely
to the desires of another soul. The problem with that
for me, as a newly married, straight-out-of-university

twenty-four-year-old, was that I was "submitting" to a lifestyle and philosophy of someone I deeply cared about, when I hadn't even identified who I was, let alone understand who he was.

Now, after thirty years of being single and not having to submit to anyone but myself, God has taken me on this journey to a place where I have to learn what true submission looks like.

The dictionary definition of *submission* is, "The action of accepting or yielding to a superior force or the will or authority of another person."

My back immediately goes up when I see words such as *superior force* or *authority*. Why should I submit to a superior force? Doesn't that connote that I am inferior? I have my own will. God has given me my own will for a purpose. Why should I submit my own will?

But when I got my thoughts out of the way, I saw that the most important words are not *superior force* or *authority* but *yielding*. Yielding means to give it away of our own free will, not under any force, not under any duress but out of love. We choose to yield.

This is what the Bible is talking about when it says in Ephesians 5:22 that wives should submit to their husbands as unto the Lord. You see, submission is given freely with love. There is absolutely no resentment in the heart of the wife when she does so, for she is yielding to the will of her husband voluntarily, not out of fear, not out of force, and clearly not out of spite (so she can tell her friends what she had to endure).

In my case, I submitted out of fear. I wanted him to love me so badly, the way I loved him, and I could not bear to see him disappointed in me in any way. I did whatever I thought he wanted, but that is not true submission. That relationship was headed for the rocks—for that reason and many others. When you are not doing you, it boomerangs, eventually.

Now, thirty years forward, I know what God designed when he made me. I have had a lot of time to figure that out— the good, the bad, and the ugly— and I'm learning that I can yield out of love without losing the essence of who I am.

Jesus yielded to death on the cross. No one took his life; he willingly laid it down out of love for you and me.

The act of submission does not stop at yielding. The Bible tells us that submission is also a plan, a playbook, to soften the hearts of unbelieving husbands (1 Peter 3:1–2). It is a salvation plan.

Submission is allowing God to transform us from the inside—the beauty of God that makes us pure and full of reverence for him; that gentle, quiet spirit that is of great worth in God's sight.

As women, we spend a great deal of money in trying to attract the right man into our lives. We take care of the outside—the hair extensions, the wigs, the false eyelashes, the false nails, the starvation diets, the body creams—all in an effort to be selected or so we can do the selecting. But Peter tells us to work just as hard on our inner selves—the unfading beauty of that gentle spirit. That is where true attraction lies for a godly man of substance.

But how does true submission impact our marriages?

If there is true submission, there is love in the home.

If there is true submission, there is less strife and fighting in the home.

If there is true submission, there is harmony in the home.

If there is true submission, the knot tied at the beginning of the marriage gets stronger.

If there is true submission, our daughters learn what that looks like and model it in their own homes.

Is there a part for husbands to play in marriage? Of course. They are to love their wives as themselves, which I think is the bigger idea than submission. There is a lot for a man to unpack in that idea.

So what is submission? Submission is yielding; it's giving up on some of your ideas or thoughts to the will of your husband in a loving manner, totally understanding that God has placed him as your head for a reason.

What does this mean, especially to our daughters, who are looking for life partners? Choose well, select a man you can respect and to whom you can yield all the days of your life; select a man who puts God first and then you.

Submission is strength.

14

Building

Nehemiah 3–4

Such a glorious day!—the wedding dress, the bridal train; the guests in their best outfits; all the well-wishers standing in line to congratulate you both; fathers and mothers beaming, totally proud of you both. After all, they are witnessing their daughter get married to a wonderful young man, soon to be their son in law. A glorious day indeed!

We get married that day with butterflies in our stomachs, and we say "I do" to all manners of things. We leave the grand ceremony with all the hope and great expectations of "happily ever after", but we fail to understand that the butterflies don't always stay on the entire journey with us. They take their leave too, like the guests. They stay a little while but eventually they leave.

The role of the butterflies is to help husband and wife bond, initially; after all, we each come from different family dynamics, which now have to be blended into the new family dynamic.

Most of us, however, are not told that this blending is hard work. The blending is what is called *marriage*, and building the marriage is primarily the work of the wife, as the husband has not played this role before. Wives, however, from when they were young, played house, played with baby dolls and dollhouses, and had pretend tea parties. This role has played out in our lives, and we have been programmed to take on the role of the builder, more so than men.

Initially, as we start to build, we turn the house into a home, a safe place. We develop a close-knit group of friends. We blend the two families together at Christmas and Thanksgiving, and the butterflies help us in keeping the strife away, as we are so in love with each other. Things go smoothly, and we are happy.

This state, however, does not often last, as pressures in marriage start to rear their heads—lack of finances, mother-in-law issues, fertility problems, dashed expectations, lack of communication, and so on.

Building is how a woman navigates her home through these pressures, while keeping those butterflies around longer than they want to be there. If effectively done, the butterflies could stay for the duration of the marriage. They might occasionally disappear but will always come back.

Nehemiah 3–4

Nehemiah was a cupbearer to King Artaxerxes. When Nehemiah learned that the walls of Jerusalem had been burned and it was in ruins, he got the king's permission to go back to Jerusalem and rebuild the walls with fellow Jews.

On starting the project of rebuilding, however, he found he had detractors, Tobiah and Sanballat, who were not happy that Nehemiah had come to promote the welfare of the Israelites.

Sometimes, when we embark on the institution of marriage, others on the outside may be looking in to see if the marriage will work or how long it takes before they see cracks in the wall. That was the case with Tobiah and Sanballat. They threw insults at the Israelites as they built the walls of Jerusalem and made fun of them. But the Israelites kept on building.

When Sanballat and Tobiah realized that their

jeering didn't stop the rebuilding, they plotted to fight the Israelites while they were building in order to stop the progress.

Sanballat and Tobiah are the pressures that rear their heads as we try to build our homes. They are subtle initially, and we pay no attention to them, believing they will go away once they see progress in the marriage. Some do, and some don't. It is the aggressive pressures, like Sanballat and Tobiah, that are determined to cause a problem to which we need to pay attention.

So how did Nehemiah and the Israelites deal with Sanballat and Tobiah? The walls of Jerusalem still needed to be built, but could they ignore those two and their plotting?

In most marriages, there is a tendency to focus on the pressures in an effort to resolve them first, thereby leaving the building process. We believe that if the problems are resolved, then we can get back to building the home. But is that the right way to deal with this? Let's examine what Nehemiah and the Israelites did.

Nehemiah 4:14–19

When the Israelites heard of Tobiah and Sanballat's plot to kill them while they were rebuilding, they were afraid, and some wanted to give up (as we do in marriages sometimes at the first sign of trouble). But Nehemiah reminded the nobles, the officials, and the rest of the Israelites of why they were doing this.

> Don't be afraid of them. Remember the Lord, who is great and awesome, and fight for your brothers, your sons, and daughters, your wives and your homes. (Nehemiah 4:14 KJV)

When you know what the fight is all about, it makes it easier to be determined to stay in the fight.

So Nehemiah devised a plan. It was an ingenious one, really. Yes, they would fight Sanballat and Tobiah, but they also would continue to rebuild. So every Israelite who was not building guarded the rebuild with a sword at hand, protecting the builders. And those who brought the building materials to the builders wore swords at their sides as they worked.

The building of the walls of Jerusalem was to continue, regardless of the plot to kill them, and the end result was that the walls of Jerusalem came right up in front of their enemies. Sanballat and Tobiah had a front-row seat to witness the favor of God on his people.

We lose our marriages because we have not learned Nehemiah's principles of building in the presence of our enemies. The Lord says to us, "I have laid a table before you in the presence of your enemies, and anointed your head with oil and your cup overflows" (Psalm 23).

We get lost in the fight and stop the building, and that is when the butterflies take their leave—they love a harmonious environment. Once they leave and we can't get them back, it becomes a slippery slope downward.

Let's teach our newly married daughters to continue to build the home, even when life's pressures occur, and to keep those butterflies with them throughout the marriage.

How do you keep the butterflies? Remember what brought you together in the first place, what you shared while dating, and the concern you had for each other's well-being, and enjoy those things again.

Here are a few things to bring the butterflies back:

- Having once-a-week date night without children
- Helping each other, in and outside of the home
- Cooking together

- Enjoying laughter together
- Creating new memories
- Enjoying great sex

Those are a few moments that can keep those butterflies hanging around while you fight the good fight of faith.

Be strong, and have faith in God.

15

Notes for My Daughter-in-Law

———◆———

Oh, how he loves you.

On Love

He is not very verbal about his feelings for you, but please don't mistake that for not loving you. He just doesn't know how to use his words to express his feelings. He will make his love known to you through those precious cards that he gives you. Read them, for he carefully selects them to speak the words that he can't.

On Friendship

Choose to be his friend first, before becoming his lover. He values friendship more than love. His friends are carefully selected, and it's important that he see you as one. True friendship, he believes, always stands the test of time.

On Children

Plan on having many kids. He will never tell you so, but he has always wished he had siblings. He's an only child, so I have failed him in that regard. Although he wants many kids, when he says *enough*, listen to him. It won't be for not wanting more but wanting to ensure that he gives the world to those he begat.

On Aloneness

Those times may be difficult for you. You may feel he is drifting. Give him that space, as the world sometimes confuses him. This is his way of safeguarding the sanctity of who he is. He will rejoin the world with a new vigor and a deep appreciation for you.

On Career

His choice of profession would never be based on the love of money but on his passion. Being the nerd that he is, he continually thinks outside the box, which is not necessarily synonymous with making the quick bucks. However, his name will be spoken in different spheres of life that others can only read about. And the money, which is not important to him, will seek him out as one searches for a precious jewel. Be patient with him as he creates. Such is his destiny.

On Money

Be the keeper of the money. He has no respect for it. He sees it as a means to reach his goals and doesn't care what he does with it, provided it gets him to his expected end. So you save, you build, you invest, and be charitable. He will be too busy changing the world to care about it.

His Friendships

His friends are carefully chosen, and his loyalty to them has no limits. As such, he has only a handful of friends. These are like-minded people whose camaraderie is not of mundane conversations but of meaningful liaisons to reach a common goal. They are comrades, seeking ways to arrive at the destiny preordained for each—almost like the Templar Knights, one could say. Do not seek to get in between them, for you may find yourself on the outside. Instead, seek to protect their journey through prayers, as they circle around life as we know it. They don't always see life the same way we do.

On Food

Cook what you like. He will always eat it and be thankful, even if it doesn't taste so good. That's his way of showing appreciation for feeding him. However, please don't misunderstand this as his inability to cook. He makes the meanest pot roast and bakes like you would not believe. He brings to cooking the same passion he brings to solving engineering problems—he treats everything like mathematical equations. Follow the equations; get the right results. That is why he is the baker in the family.

On Health and Wellness

Look after yourself and eat right—not too many carbohydrates; lots of fruits and vegetables. Exercise as often as you can, and always look like a million bucks. He will always appreciate you for this. Buy the best clothes, drive the best car, keep the best home, be in heels all the time, and stay slim. In other words, give him a reason to look at you twice. He will say nothing, but his heart will be content. All I have asked of you comes naturally to him. Be his match! *Fat* is not in his dictionary. He cannot comprehend fat, and this is tantamount to grounds for divorce in his world. Be well; he needs you for this journey.

On Family

When there is conflict in your family, don't expect him to take sides. This he will not do. It doesn't mean that he doesn't care about your side of things, even when you are completely right. It is his way of saying that he loves you, and loving you means loving your family as well. He will not get between the two. He is not prepared to lose you or your love.

On Me

His love for me runs deep, but he knows the place the two great loves of his life occupy in his heart. He will not trade one for the other. But instead, he will seek to ensure his "choice" works in concert with his "need". His and my love of independence probably will mean that we won't all live in the same house, but he will never seek to be too far from me. This is to ensure that he keeps his God-given mandate—to protect and care for me.

On God and Christianity

He is a man of science and believes in the logic of the mind. However, he has come to love and trust God. He may not seem like it when you meet him, and he may snigger at you if you become fanatical, but when he prays, he is betrayed by the words of his mouth. His eloquent manner of praying and the deep thoughts attached to his words in prayer reveal the depth of his love for God and God's sovereignty in his life. He is still growing in his faith, as God has not yet fully revealed himself to him.

You be the woman of God that you are, and continue in faith when he falters, as we all do from time to time. Be steadfast and unwavering in your love for God and for him, and through you, he will have that experiential knowledge of who God is—that knowledge that stays with you through mountaintop-and-valley times in life.

Well, my daughter-in-law, I don't know who you are, but I do hope one day you will read this and smile.

And in good time, when you have mastered all the above, you will have become my daughter.

With all my love,

Mum

16

Creation

———◆———

Genesis 1:1–31

The creativity of God is written in Genesis 1. It states how our God created the heavens and the earth. But today, I read it with fresh eyes. I see how systematic and deliberate our God was in creation. He is not a God of confusion. He did not throw everything in at once and hope for the best. On every day of the six days of creation, he started with the larger picture and then slowly added the details, like a seasoned artist. But the most important thing our God did was to stop at the end of each day of creation, step back to look at the work of his hands, and assess it. The Bible tells us that his conclusion at the end of each day was that it was good.

The creation on the sixth day was the creation of both male and female. That was the only one for which God consulted with others, as to how to make this wonderful creation—man!

> Then God said, "Let us make man in our own image, in our likeness, and let them rule over fish of the sea, and the birds in the air, over livestock, over all the earth, and over all creatures that move along the ground." (Genesis 1:26 KJV)

On the previous five days of creation before then, God solely decided on his creation, but when it came to man, he paused, consulted, and worked with others to create us. The Bible is silent about who the "*us*" is in "Let us make man in our own image," but my guess is that the others are the Son and the Holy Spirit.

I think about the beauty all around us that we see and may take for granted. If we could only stop and take it in, we would stand in awe and amazement of the creative power of God. He was in awe of it! He stood at the end of each day, took it all in and said it was good!.

As mentioned, the Bible tells us that they chose to

make man in their own image, so let's delve into the meaning of *image*.

Image means likeness, resemblance, depiction, or representation. From this definition, we see that we were made in God's likeness, his resemblance, his representation. How awesome is that! Think about it—in everyone, therein lies the creative power of God.

Have you ever wondered why some people come into this world and completely transform our world from what we know it to be—people such as Steve Jobs, Bill Gates, Richard Branson, Mark Zuckerberg, and Thomas Edison? It's not that they have special powers or that they're different from you and I. They, however, have tapped into—knowingly or unknowingly—that which is already in them: the creative power of God.

A lot of us don't know what we have in us because we don't ask God, "What have you put inside me that I need to birth forth into this earth?" Trust me; it is in there. We just need to probe and be willing to explore.

Creativity comes in different forms for different people. Our God is a God of diversification and what he has placed inside of me may be completely different from what he has placed in you. He is waiting for us to ask him to help unlock the gift, the talent, the creativity he has in us. Some have found other ways to unlock this creative power, but we know the God of creation, so why don't we go to him? He knows our potential and what he put in us when he created us.

Our God wants us to use the talent he has given each one of us and to multiply the talents. God talks about seed-bearing plants on the face of the earth that he has given to us. The fact that the plant has seeds tells me that the plant is supposed to multiply. Our God is a God of increase, which is why, when he gives us a talent or creativity, he expects us to increase and multiply the talent for the benefit of others.

Remember the parable of the master who left his servants with a certain number of talents per servant before leaving for a journey. When he came back and asked his servants what they had done with the talents, two of the servants had increased the talents by putting them to work, but the third servant had dug a hole in the ground and buried his talents. So instead of putting his talents to work, he hid them underground. Instead of putting them in the bank to at least accrue some interest, he hid them in the ground. So the master took those talents and gave them to the one servant who had made most of the talents given to him (Matthew 25:14–28).

So it is with our God. He has placed this creativity and talent in us so we can grow and multiply it. If we believe only that we have the same creative power of God working in us, then we can transform our lives and the lives of others.

Mothers, let's encourage our children to explore everything good—music, writing, painting, singing, dancing, gaming—not just school curriculum of math, science, and English. Let's allow our children to be curious right from birth and even during pregnancy. Expose the fetus to different kinds of music. Fetuses that listen to classical music in their mothers' wombs turn out to be intelligent human beings.

For us parents, let's not think that we are too old to learn something new—another creative thing to do. Creativity never stops or dies. It lies dormant in us, waiting for us to come knocking at its door. So learn a new instrument, write a poem, pick up a paintbrush, start a coaching class, write an editorial—do something.

There is more in you than you know—a whole lot more!

17

The Power of God.

Exodus 3–5

Our God is a holy God who desires for us to worship him in reverence. He is an exacting God. He knows precisely how he wants us to do things, especially in worship to him. When it comes to instructions to us, he is very precise and expects that we will follow his instructions as he lays it out to us.

In Exodus 3:2–6, Moses gets introduced to the God of Abraham, Isaac, and Jacob. God's first words to Moses were for him to take off his shoes, as the ground he stood on was holy. God demands our reverence in worship of him. He is a powerful God and needs us to understand that.

Throughout the Bible, we find instances of human

beings going against God's instructions. God's immediate reaction to disobedience is to strike us dead (Thank God for Jesus, who sits at the right hand of God, interceding on our behalf.)

In Acts 5:1–6, Ananias and Sapphira promised the proceeds from the sale of their property to the early church; then they decided to keep some of the proceeds for themselves and lie about it to the congregation. God did not take that lightly, and both husband and wife were struck down instantly.

In 2 Samuel 6:6, David and his men, one of whom was Uzzah, were transporting the ark of the covenant. One of God's instructions on transporting the ark was that the ark was not to be touched by any man. However, as the ark was about to fall during the transportation, Uzzah touched it to support it, and he was struck dead instantly.

This informs me that God's instructions must be carried out precisely, regardless of whether we feel he needs our help. God is *God*! He does not need our help, and neither does he need us to be unfaithful or disloyal.

I've read about Moses, the leader of the Israelites out of Egypt—the one who brought about all those plagues in Egypt in the presence of the great pharaoh, the one who divided the Red Sea. Yes, that Moses.

Did you know that God almost killed him before he went on the journey to rescue the Israelites out of Egypt? (Exodus 4:24–27).

When I read that, I thought, *Why would God want to kill him after he had just given him instructions for dealing with the Israelites and Pharaoh?* God gave Moses a preview of what was going to happen. Moses was in a good place. He had spoken to God and received instructions on how to lead his people out of four hundred years of bondage. Why kill him on his way to carry out God's own will? I had to go back to Exodus 4:14–17 to find the answer to that question.

Our God is a powerful God, and he demands our reverence and obedience. When God met with Moses at the burning bush, he told Moses of his plans to use him to rescue his children out of Egypt. God was met with a very reluctant man who had a whole load of excuses for why he was not the man for the job. God was patient with Moses, and for every objection that Moses gave, God showed him how to overcome it. But Moses wouldn't stop with his objections. The Bible says, "The Lord's anger burned against Moses." When Moses said he had never been eloquent in speaking to people, God said, "What about allowing your brother Aaron, the Levite, to speak for you?"

What Moses failed to understand was that God

is not man with whom to negotiate your way out of doing his will. When God gives you instructions, you execute them and leave it to him to figure out all the ins and outs of getting the job done.

Why did God want to kill Moses? After all, he had just told him that Aaron could now speak for Moses with the Israelites and with Pharaoh.

> He [Aaron] will speak to the people for you and it will be as if he were your mouth, and as if you were *God* to him. (Exodus 4:16 KJV, italics added)

And therein lies the issue. This is exactly what God wanted from Moses—to be his God and use Moses's mouth as his mouthpiece—but Moses declined. And in so doing, Moses took on the role of God in Aaron's life and used Aaron as his own mouthpiece.

Remember God's commandment: "There shall be no other God before me for I am a jealous God" (Exodus 20:3 KJV).

Moses had just broken that commandment unintentionally. (The Ten Commandments were not in existence then. That came later, but we have an unchanging God.) God then decided to kill Moses on his way back to Egypt. Moses, however, was saved by Zipporah, a lady with whom Moses stayed with on his journey back to Egypt. Zipporah circumcised her son and took the foreskin and touched Moses's feet with it.

I believe that with Zipporah's actions and the shedding of the blood, she presented a sin offering to God for Moses's mistake and thereby saved Moses's life.

Moses's life was spared but only for a while because Moses still did not know that the God he was serving was an all-powerful and all-holy God who demanded that his instructions must be obeyed.

Numbers 20:10–13 tells us that after Moses led the Israelites out of Egypt and into the desert, the Israelites became thirsty and cried out for water. God told Moses to speak to the rock at Meribah in front of the people, and the rock would pour out its waters. But instead, Moses struck the rock twice because God previously had instructed him to do that at a different place and time and also because Moses was angry at the rebellious Israelites.

Due to this disobedience, God told Moses, "Because you did not trust me enough to honor me as holy in the sight of the Israelites, you will not bring this community into the land that I give them" (Numbers 20:12 NLT). Moses died without getting to the Promised Land.

It is of the utmost importance that we understand that *God is not man.* His words and instructions are Law. Sometimes, we do not understand his reasons or plans, but who are we to undermine his authority or instruction? We are his creation, and our whole purpose is to serve him and let his will be done, here on earth as it is in heaven.

Let us, therefore, strive to listen keenly for his instructions, as mothers, regarding our homes, our children, our families, our neighbors, our jobs—all areas of our lives—and do as he has instructed. Obey God, and leave everything else to him. He surely will bring everything to bear fruit in our lives.

> Trust God with all your heart, Lean not on your own understanding. In all your ways acknowledge him and he will direct your path.
> —Proverbs 3:5–6 (KJV)

18

The End-Times

Revelation 1–2

The times we are in right now seem so dangerous to our minds and souls. It seems to me that the world is going through a phase of admonition from the Lord, and instead of recognizing it for what it is and repenting of our wicked ways, we are pointing fingers at one another.

As of this writing, COVID-19 is running rampant all over the world, like a bad wind. It's a virus we can't see, we can't treat, and we can't hide from that has stopped the entire world in its tracks and has forced us to separate ourselves from our loved ones.

As if that were not enough to deal with, we watched the brutal killing of a black man in America by a white police officer, who knelt on his throat while the man pleaded with the officer not to kill him; four other white police officers—those who are instructed to protect society—stood by watching as the man was killed.

All this played out on our televisions like a bad reality TV show. The result of this killing led to riots, protests, and looting in America, with Black Lives Matter protests throughout the world, much like the virus—a bad wind.

They say things come in threes, so we wait with bated breath for the third event. What is it? I'm not sure, but it is coming.

The events at this time led me to read the book of Revelation. There have been many talks about this being the end-time, as referred to in the Bible. I don't know if this is the end-time or not—the Bible says no one knows the time or day that the Lord will return—but there are clear indications in the world that things are not right, and individuals have become lovers of themselves. It's everyone for himself or herself, and don't remember your neighbor. This culture has become so ingrained in us that we can't tell what is right from what is wrong.

In Revelation 1 and 2, a vision was given to John for the seven churches. These first two chapters deal with visions or warnings to three of the seven churches. The theme in all three visions was the same—what they were doing right, what they were doing wrong, and what they would receive if they repented and did the will of God.

I also discovered that God sent his angels to guard each church, just as he has an angel assigned to each one of us. "For he will command his angels concerning you, to guard you in all your ways" (Psalm 91:11 KJV). They are there to protect us and to do God's will in our lives. However, they are obedient to God and God's words, not to us. This means that God can call them back from their missions to protect us. When God does that, we experience calamity, as Job did. Job experienced calamity because God removed the hedge of protection around Job's life in an experiment that took place between God and Satan.

Now that we know that God can remove his hedge of protection around the world and tell his angels to stand back, I believe this is what the world is experiencing right now. The *Watchers*, as the angels are called, have been given instruction to stand back, and now Satan and his demons are running amuck, blowing the wind of destruction all over the world.

Why would God do that?

When men shut out God and become lovers of themselves and are full of pride.

When men do not care about their fellow human beings because of their skin color.

When men delve into all manner of sexual impurity and immorality and call it alternative lifestyle or sexual preference.

When men begin to think and behave as if they are gods and not created beings.

The Bible tells us that God removes himself from humans and leaves us to the depravity of our minds, such as we are seeing in our world today.

But there's a way out of all of this,

> If my people, who are called by name, would humble themselves, pray and seek my face, and turn from their wicked ways, then I will hear from heaven and will forgive their sin and heal their land. (2 Chronicles 7:14 NIV)

Here's the thing: as a people, we need to recognize that we are in trouble. As far as I can tell, we are not there yet. We are still pointing fingers and still saying, I'm not wearing a mask for you because:

- I can't get infected. I'm young.
- I don't believe in COVID-19.
- I have a business to run.

- It only majorly affects black people.
- I have an election to win.
- I have to celebrate my birthday.

There are other thoughts, such as:

- You are black; therefore, you are two-thirds of a human being.
- You are a bus driver or janitor, so you need no respect from me.
- I have COVID-19, so everyone else must get it. No isolation for me.

Or worse still,

- I will cough on or lick all grocery products at the store.

There are also other school of thoughts, such as:

- You appear to be richer than me, so I will steal from you what I can, even when you treat me well.
- I will sell witchcraft wares online with wicked intentions on another human being. (I saw that trending last week.)
- You are black, so I will pay you less than your white counterpart, even though you both do the same job.

Until we all recognize the evil that we have become as a society and call for a worldwide repentance, turning away from our wicked ways, I believe the other shoe is about to drop, and it will be bigger still in its devastation. That is the only way God can get our attention.

The good news, however, is that God does not turn a deaf ear to our pleas. If we repent and seek his face, he is willing and able to forgive us and heal our land.

Revelation 1 and 2 tell us that those who overcome will be rewarded. Those who heed God's warning and repent will be rewarded.

> Remember the height from which you have fallen! Repent and do the things you did at first. If you do not repent, I will come to you and remove your lampstands. [lampstands are churches] from its places. (Rev. 2:5 KJV)

The brick-and-mortar churches are gone temporarily, but thank God for the online churches.

If we choose to repent, below are some of the ways God will reward us:

I will give you the right to eat from the "Tree of Life" [eternal life] which is in the paradise of God. (Rev 2:7 KJV)

He who overcomes will not be hurt at all by the second death. (Rev 2:11 KJV)

I will give you some of the hidden manna [hidden provision of God]. I will also give him a white stone with a new name written on it known only to him who receives it. (Rev 2:17 KJV)

To him who overcomes and does my will to the end, I will give authority over the nations. (KJV)

I have deviated from only talking to women. As important as we women are in the scheme of things, this one speaks to all of us—men, women, husbands, wives, uncles, aunts, daughters, sons, employers, employees, presidents, prime ministers, queens, kings, pastors, priests, and evangelicals.

We all need to bend our knees in prayer and repent of our wicked ways, that God may hear us from heaven and heal our land.

May God help us all. Amen.

19

Understanding God's Passion

Luke 1

Have you ever wondered what the difference was between the two outcomes of angel Gabriel's visits to Zechariah and to Mary? Why was Zechariah struck dumb, and Mary was left to speak? After all, both received good news from angel Gabriel with regards to the birth of a baby.

Angel Gabriel is the foremost angel in heaven, and he tells Zechariah that he "stands in the presence of God." He delivers good news to Zechariah, saying that Elizabeth, his barren wife, was going to bear him a son, though she had been barren for a while.

In the same time frame, angel Gabriel goes to a virgin named Mary and tells her that the Holy Spirit is going to come upon her, and she will be pregnant with a son, though she was only newly engaged to Joseph and had not married him yet.

Obviously, both declarations seemed impossible to Zechariah and Mary because of the apparent impediments, and both expressed this to angel Gabriel.

So why was Zechariah struck with dumbness, and Mary was allowed to continue speaking?

This is where understanding God's passion comes into play. The knowledge of God's passion brings about a total and complete trust in his prophetic words, given to us by his angels through visions and through direct utterances to us.

God's passion is *Love*. He is *Love*!

> For, God so Loved the world, that he gave his only begotten son, that whosoever believes in him shall not perish but have everlasting life. (John 3:16 NIV)

This has been God's plan and purpose all along—to dwell with humankind.

Adam and Eve were created for that purpose, before the fall of man in Eden. The plan of redemption came out of that love to bring us back to that original idea, that original plan.

In understanding this passion of God, we realize that all he wants us to do is to trust in him, because we know that he loves us implicitly; to trust him, even when an angel comes our way and tells us of things to come that seem totally unbelievable to us.

The Bible tells us to be like children when it comes to trusting God. Children will believe anything their parents tell them—the Tooth Fairy, Santa Claus, the Easter Bunny and all other mythical characters we have fed them over time. They love us, so they trust us, and therefore they believe us, at least till they find out differently.

God wants the same from us—that childlike trust, the trust that comes from a love for God.

Now going back to the different outcomes of angel Gabriel's visits to Zechariah and Mary.

In examining Mary's response, we have to look at the intensity of belief and trust that is required of her.

- She was a virgin and had known no man (had no sexual interaction with any man).
- She was recently engaged to Joseph.
- She had never heard of anyone becoming impregnated by the Holy Spirit—by the way, neither had the entire world.
- She had friends and family who were aware of her upcoming wedding to Joseph.

How, in any world, past or present, does anyone wrap his or her mind around such a proclamation, let alone believe it and—worst of all—explain it to your fiancé, families, and friends.

Mary, however, was special. She understood God's passion and his love for the world, and therefore, she totally trusted the words of God that came through Gabriel.

She did what any of us would do and asked, "How will this be, since I am a virgin?" She didn't say, "This cannot be possible"; or "Am I dreaming?"; or "God can't really be saying that."

Instead, her question was that of an acceptance that God had said it, so it would be done. She merely wanted to know how the process would work.

How do we know this was her attitude? The answer lies in Luke 1:38;

> "I am the Lord's servant," Mary answered." May it be to me as you have said." And with that answer Angel Gabriel left. (KJV)

Let's contrast that to Zechariah's response to the news that Elizabeth, his barren wife, was going to have a baby. The faith and trust required here to believe angel Gabriel was nowhere as intense as what was required of Mary. After all, this had already happened in his history, when Abraham's wife, Sarah, had Isaac, way into her old age, at a time when it had ceased to be with her in the manner of a child-bearing woman.

So it was not far-fetched or too much of a stretch for Zechariah to believe the good news from angel Gabriel. But Zechariah was struggling to understand God's passion, God's love for the people he created. How do we know this?

Angel Gabriel did not just tell Zechariah that his wife was going to have a child; he also told him what the child's mission would be here on earth.

> And many of the people of Israel will he bring back to the Lord [redemption], And he will go before the Lord in the spirit of Elijah, to turn the hearts of fathers to their children and the disobedient to the wisdom of the righteous. To make ready a people prepared for the Lord. (Luke 1:16–17 KJV)

However, Zechariah's heart was betrayed by the words of his mouth. "Out of the abundance of the heart, the mouth speaks" (Luke 6:45 KJV).

His words to the angel showed a lack of trust when he said, "How can I be sure of this? I am an old man, and my wife is well along in years."

And because angel Gabriel saw the distrust that came from Zechariah's heart, he struck him with dumbness, and he was unable to speak or tell others of his visitation. He had to sit on the sidelines and watch God do what only he can do. God was not about to allow Zechariah to disrupt his plans with his unbelief. So God silenced him till the work was completed and Elizabeth bore a son, whom they named John (John the Baptist), just as the angel had pronounced.

Why dumbness, though? The only reason I can think of is, "The power of life and death is in the tongue" (Proverbs 18:21 KJV). God had spoken life, but Zechariah, if left with a working tongue, was about to pronounce death.

So mothers, daughters, and all women, let us not be quick to dismiss our visions and visitations from God, especially if what we are being told to do or what we are told will happen will help the world.

Let's be like Mary and say to the Lord, I am the Lord's servant. May it be as you have said.

20

Mary Magdalene

The Controversial Woman

What happens when you are doing what comes naturally to you and history deems you a controversial figure?

Mary Magdalene was such a figure. History deemed her as controversial, perhaps because it couldn't place the role she played during Jesus's time or ministry. Or perhaps it plainly refused to acknowledge her role.

Mary Magdalene came from the city of Magdala. Her last name was not Magdalene; she was simply referred to as Mary, the Magdalene.

In biblical history, Mary has been portrayed in several roles. She was:

- the woman from whom Jesus drove out seven demons;
- the woman who was caught in an adulterous situation and was about to be stoned to death;
- the sinful woman who wiped Jesus's feet with her hair and washed it with her tears;
- a wealthy woman who was a disciple of Jesus and who supported his ministry;
- a woman who was the first to see the risen Jesus after his crucifixion;
- a woman who was by the side of Mary, the mother of Jesus, at Jesus's crucifixion;
- a woman who was said by some to have been Jesus's wife and who bore him children.

Why was Mary so controversial, and why was her role in Christianity mired in so much negative controversy? After all, many other women in biblical history had defined roles and have been acknowledged for their contributions in the Bible—women such as Mary, the mother of Jesus; Esther; Ruth; the Samaritan woman; the woman with the issue of blood, and so on.

So who was Mary Magdalene?

There are certain undeniable truths that we know about Mary.

- She was a follower of Jesus and his teachings.
- She was quite close to Jesus's family. She was at his crucifixion with his mother.
- She was in the upper room with the other disciples of Jesus. Peter and the rest of the disciples knew her by name. She was not lost in the crowd that followed Jesus.
- She was the first person to whom Jesus appeared after he had risen.
- When other disciples discovered that Jesus's body was no longer in the tomb where he'd been buried, they left and returned home, but Mary stayed back at the tomb and wept bitterly, looking for Jesus's body.
- Mary referred to Jesus as *rabboni*, meaning "teacher."

In life, when you are seen as controversial, it means you are probably doing something different, out of the norm. You are doing the unexpected or unexplainable or are causing others to think differently about certain situations. When you are controversial, you cause divisions among people. Some would agree with you and understand where you are coming from, and some will think you have lost your mind. But the one thing that is common to both factions is that they will talk about you. And Mary was certainly talked about in the Bible.

Mary was a trailblazer. Let's start with the fact that she was a woman who didn't believe that she did not have a voice in an era where women were supposed to be seen and not heard. She made herself important enough to be reckoned with by Jesus and the other disciples. The Bible is not specific about how she achieved this, but we do know it happened, as the Bible makes references to her in the midst of the other disciples and with Jesus.

Mary was a woman of great faith in Jesus and his teachings. She was regarded as a follower of Jesus. This meant she devoted her time to being wherever he was preaching. Jesus had become her teacher. You only call someone a teacher when that person is teaching you on a regular basis, and you believe in that person's teachings.

Mary was a caring woman. We know this because she had become a companion to Jesus's mother. She cared enough about Jesus and his mother to be at Jesus's crucifixion. And when she went to the tomb where Jesus was buried and discovered that the body was no longer there, she raced back to get the other disciples to come and see the empty tomb. When the others left the empty tomb, the Bible says, she hung around the tomb and wept till Jesus appeared to her. Did her tears move Jesus to reveal himself to her, thereby making her the first person to see the resurrected Jesus? Did he see the depths of her dedication to him?

Mary was a strong character. It took strength of character to be well respected by men as a woman disciple and still have a voice.

Mary was different from the women of her time. She was willing to step out for who and what she believed in. She was willing to be vilified and portrayed differently through the biblical lens of time. She was comfortable sitting with the men in the upper room with Jesus. She dared to believe that she had a role to play in the early church, though she was a woman.

For this, she was labeled a prostitute, a sinful woman, Jesus's wife, and so on. But here we are, over two thousand years later, reading about her in the Bible, and we all know her by name—Mary of Magdalene.

Where there is a greater purpose, women, let's dare to break out of the box, the mold, the thoughts and ideas that have us caged in, so that our granddaughters and great-granddaughters may someday read about us and call us by our names.

21

The Samaritan Woman

The Thirsty Woman
John 4:4

What makes the Samaritan woman the thirsty woman? The Bible tells us that at Jacob's well, she wanted the water that Jesus told her about, which would never make her go thirsty again—the living water. The Samaritan woman believed this to be a physical body of water that she could drink, but Jesus was talking about a spiritual water—the living God.

The Samaritan woman had been thirsty long before meeting Jesus. He recognized this thirst in her, even before she knew she was thirsty. How do we know she was thirsty before meeting Jesus? The

Bible tells us that she had been married five times and currently was in another "complicated" relationship.

When a woman (or man) marries five times, she or he is looking for something that can stop the feeling of dissatisfaction. Her soul was thirsty and longing for satisfaction. She did not know what was missing in her soul, but she kept going from relationship to relationship in an effort to stop this longing, this despair that swelled the feeling of thirst in her life.

When we read about the Samaritan woman, we may judge her as being a morally loose, promiscuous woman because she had many husbands, but—quite the contrary—this was a woman in search of satiety. Something was missing in her soul, but she attributed this missing connection to something a husband could give her, so she went from husband to husband.

When Jesus met her at the well, he recognized this immediately. The significance of the well does not go unnoticed, as the conversation started out from a place of a spiritual thirst at a physical well.

As the conversation goes back and forth between the Samaritan woman and Jesus, we see the juxtaposition of the spiritual against the physical. The Samaritan woman discussed water and thirst, based on her limitations as a physical being, but Jesus spoke of her thirst from a spiritual perspective. And though time was spent to assure her that she was speaking to the Messiah, the Savior of the world, she could only refer to Jesus as a prophet.

In life, we are limited by our physical existence, and we view all things through our limitations. But as we endeavor to renew our minds through studying the Word of God and praying for spiritual understanding and wisdom, God reveals spiritual thoughts and revelations to us.

Why was this meeting between Jesus and the Samaritan woman so important that it was documented in the Bible?

We do know that the Samaritans and the Jews were not friendly and did not associate with one another, let alone a Jewish man speaking to a Samaritan woman. Yet Jesus stayed by Jacob's well and waited for this Samaritan woman to come so they could have this conversation. Why?

We know that she did not recognize him as her Savior, even when Jesus told her all about her life. She thought he was a prophet of some sort, and she said to Jesus, "I know that the Messiah is coming. When he comes, he will explain everything to us" (John 4:25 KJV).

The one thing the Samaritan woman had going for

her was that she knew how to bring people together and make them listen to her.

The Bible tells us that when Jesus told her that he was that Messiah, she left her water jar at the well and went into town to tell people to come and see a man (not the Messiah) who had told her everything that she had ever done. Could this be the Messiah? She still was quite unsure of who this Jesus was.

Because this Samaritan woman had the gift of persuasion, the Bible tells us that the people of the town followed her back to the well to meet Jesus.

A lot of Samaritans believed in the Lord that day because of the testimony of the Samaritan woman at the well. They listened to Jesus and persuaded him to spend a few days with them, and many more believed because they had Jesus in their midst.

Why was this meeting documented in the Bible? Though we do not know the Samaritan woman by name, her thirst was instrumental in bringing many Samaritans to the Lord, for the Lord had quenched her thirst. Jesus waited for her by the well, knowing full well the role she would play in the lives of her people and in the spreading of the gospel throughout Samaria.

As women, we all have various thirsts in our lives that only God can satiate. Let's not look to quench that thirst through other means, such as sex, alcohol, drugs, overindulgence, numerous husbands, gluttony, and so forth. Let's search for our God who quenches all thirst by providing us with his living water.

22

Vindication

Psalm 24, 37

Injustice! Injustice!, we cry out. How can he do this to me? How can she do this to me? After all I've been through with him? After all I have done for her?

Many of us have either said those words or have heard others say them. The words come from a place of deep hurt and despair. The emotions behind those words are real and the pain is often completely unbearable.

These words normally come when a promise has been broken, a vow has been cast aside, a friendship lost, or even when there's been a betrayal. We are left with the fragments of what used to be a wholesome relationship or partnership. And we watch as our lives are shattered into fragments, while the other party sails away into a happily-ever-after life.

This is not an unusual situation; it's even more prevalent than one might think. The situation arises because we are human beings with thoughts, experiences, morals, ethics, and decisions. The degree of any one of those human traits determines how often we fall into this gut-wrenching scenario. By that I mean, how deeply do you think? What have your past experiences taught you? What morals do you have? What are your business ethics? Or are ethics for the simple-minded?

These are questions we need to ask ourselves so we don't make promises or vows to another person that we can't keep. What checks and balances have we put in place to ensure we keep our word?

Today, I'm writing to the pained soul—the one whose anger and disappointment has bloomed into revenge; the one who would do anything to get back at the perpetrator. Yes, it's to you I write.

I understand that pain that engulfs you. It incapacitates you, but it can destroy you if left unattended, for it eats you up from within. The reason we feel this pain is because we believe in the balance of scales. We believe if we have been good to someone, that person should be good to us. If I give you my all, you should do the same for me. If I have invested in you, I should see the returns and receive them.

But our mistake is in thinking that life is fair; it's not. There are no balanced scales. Even God does not promise us a life devoid of pain. What he says is, *Carry your cross and follow me.* God does not promise a balanced scale, but hates a rigged scale—the one that is rigged against you from the get-go. You never had a chance with that scale, and that is the scale that God comes out against. With all other life scales, it is what it is.

If we know this, how do we deal with the pain of rejection, of adultery, of divorce, of death, of loss of a relationship, of deceit, of broken business deals, of back-stabbing, and so on? As Christians, how do we deal with this pain? This is when we go into the Word of God to find comfort and solace. The first thing that God wants to assure us is that he is a mighty warrior, and he will fight for us.

> Who is this King of Glory? The Lord is strong and mighty. The Lord mighty in battle. (Psalm 24:8 KJV)

God wants us to know that we need not seek revenge; we should be still, believe him, and trust him to vindicate us.

Be still before the Lord and wait patiently
for him. Do not fret when they succeed
in their ways, when they carry out their
wicked schemes. (Psalm 37:7 KJV)

God promises you that they will not get away
with whatever they have done to you and with the
measure of wickedness they perpetrated toward you,
so shall the measure of God's response be to their
wickedness.

The wicked draw the sword and bend the
bow, to bring down the poor and needy
to slay those whose ways are upright.
But their swords will pierce their own
hearts and their bows will be broken.
(Psalm 37:14–15 KJV)

But what does God require from us in order to go
into battle for us? He sees our pain, but if we take
matters into our own hands, will he still go into battle
for us?

Who may ascend the hill of the Lord?
Who may stand in his holy place? [That
is, to petition the Lord on our behalf.] He
who has clean hands (the person has not

repaid evil for evil) and a pure heart, who does not lift up his soul to an idol or swear by what is false. He will receive blessings from the Lord and VINDICATION from God his Saviour. (Psalm 24:3–5 KJV)

We want to wait on the Lord for his vindication, but it's hard to wait on him. We want to see vindication right now, but God's ways are not our ways, and his timing is his alone. What do we do while we wait for him to vindicate us?

Delight yourself in the Lord and he will give you the desires of your heart. Commit your way to the Lord, trust him and he will do this. (Psalm 37:15 KJV)

Will we get a reward for trusting him with our pain; for letting him vindicate us for being obedient to his Word?

The earth is the Lord's and everything in it. The world and all who live in it. (Psalm 24:1 KJV)

A little while and the wicked will be no more, and though you look for them, they will not be found, But the meek shall inherit the land and enjoy great peace. (Psalm 37:10–11 KJV)

Those the Lord blesses will inherit the land. (Psalm 37:22 KJV)

The righteous will inherit the land and dwell in it forever. (Psalm 37:29 KJV)

Wait for the Lord and keep his ways. He will exalt you to inherit the Land. (Psalm 37:34 KJV)

So after all is said and done, it's better by far to take our pain to the Lord and let him fight our battles for us and vindicate us, while preparing us to inherit the land.

23

The Woman with the Issue of Blood

The Desperate Woman
Matthew 9:20–22; Mark 5:25–24; Luke 8:43–48

In the Bible, a story is not always repeated in all the gospels unless it is a significant story. The Woman with the Issue of Blood was such a story, repeated by Matthew, Mark, and Luke. This is a simple story, really. A woman who had constant bleeding for twelve years (dysmenorrhea) touched the garment of Jesus and was healed. Why is this story more significant than all the other healings Jesus did? Let's take a look at this woman, whose name we're not told but who had a dire situation.

The Bible tells us that this woman had been hemorrhaging blood for twelve years. In that culture at that time, when a woman had her period, she was said to be unclean and needed to separate herself from people. Because this woman continually bled for twelve years, she literally had been in self-isolation for that length of time.

Due to the COVID-19 pandemic, we all know how isolation feels. We likely complained because we were told to keep to ourselves for two months, and now, many of us blatantly refuse any more isolation because we are tired of not socializing with family, friends, and colleagues. Now, imagine twelve years of self-isolation, which is what the woman with the issue of blood went through, and what her state of mind was like.

The Bible tells us that she had visited many doctors and had spent all her money looking for a cure. This shows how desperate she was, trying to rid herself of this illness. The illness had taken control of her life, of who she was, of her social status, and of all things that mattered to her.

In life, people are hemorrhaging, perhaps not blood, as she was, but in other areas of their lives; there are situations that are killing them, and they don't seem to have any solution to their problem. And very much like the woman with the issue of blood, money does not solve or stop the hemorrhaging. What are we willing to do to get help?

The woman with the issue of blood heard that Jesus was around and chose to go in search of him, perhaps risking being stoned. She went into a crowd of that size—one large enough to press against Jesus—yet she was not worried about what could possibly happen to her if they found out who she was—the woman with the issue of blood.

What level of desperation drives us not to consider our own lives in order to fix our problems?

I considered why the woman did not just go to Jesus and say, "Here I am; please heal me." Instead, she thought to herself, *If only I could touch the hem of his garment, I know I would be healed.*

To go to Jesus, she would have had to declare to him—and everyone else—that she was that woman who had been locked away from society for twelve years because she was unclean. Perhaps she feared stigmatization, that people would know who she was and never let her live it down.

We all are very good at hiding our problems. We slap on a smile and carry on because we don't want anyone to talk about us, make fun of us, or—worse still—ostracize us.

The one thing the woman with the issue of blood had going for her was that she was bold, and she believed. Her boldness gave her the courage to touch

Jesus's garment, and her belief assured her that she would be made whole if she touched him.

When we have a persistent nagging, hemorrhaging problem, do we give up and say it's the will of God for us, or are we like the woman with the issue of blood, seeking God with a fervent belief that he can make us whole again if we touch him?

Let's unpack Jesus's response to being touched. Remember that Jesus was on a mission to heal the daughter of Jairus, the ruler of the synagogue. He was also among a large crowd that was pressing against him. But when this woman touched him, he felt her. The Bible says that power immediately left his body. What made Jesus feel her touch and not the touch of all the others who were pressing against him? When Jesus asked who had touched him, his disciples probably thought, *What are you talking about? Everyone is pressed up against you; everyone is touching you.* But Jesus clarified the touch and said, "No, this is different. Power has left my body." So what made the woman's touch powerful enough to draw power from Jesus? Was it her profound belief? Or was it her long-standing situation? Whatever it was, it stopped Jesus from continuing on his mission to Jairus's house. Jesus stopped for her.

Now let's say that you are the woman with

the issue of blood, who had sneakily touched the garment of Jesus, hoping to get away with it without his knowledge. Then he calls you out and says, "Who has done this?" Your heart starts racing, your palms are sweaty, and you are so afraid, but you come out to be identified. The fear of being identified by the crowd has now come to roost, and you are made public for the world to see. Your secret issue now is displayed openly for all to see. But the Savior of the world says to you, "Daughter, your faith has healed you. Go in peace."

Imagine the joy that fills your heart at that moment. Twelve years of the pain of isolation, of lack of love from family and friends, of wasted funds, of ostracization and stigmatization all disappears in that very moment.

Only Jesus can bring such absolute conclusions to our desperation. Let's seek him and him only for persistent issues in our lives.

Do not give up to the temptation of giving in. Be bold enough to touch his garment by your faith in him.

Her faith put an end to her desperation!

24

Hannah

The Praying Woman
1 Samuel 1–2

How do we pray effective prayers—the kind of prayers that make God reverse his position on decisions he's already made?

Hannah, the second wife of Elkanah, was barren. Her barrenness was not due to a twist of nature or a medical problem. The Bible says that God closed off Hannah's womb because her husband, Elkanah, loved her more than his other wife, Peniniah. Elkanah favored Hannah over Peniniah when sharing meat on the day of sacrificing to the Lord.

Elkanah's first mistake was not realizing that God wanted everyone to have equal opportunity to worship him. When Elkanah gave double portions of meat for sacrifice to Hannah and just enough to Peniniah and her children because he loved Hannah more, Elkanah was effectively saying to Hannah that her prayers should matter more to God than Peniniah's.

However, that is not how God operates. He is a just God, and he wants us all to have the same access to him.

That is why, as created beings, we all have two legs, two arms, and one head. If he gave some of us three legs and others two heads, those with two legs and one head would feel God had dealt with them badly, that the scales had been rigged against them from the outset.

As for Hannah's barrenness, the Bible tells us that it brought her much pain and sorrow. Peniniah kept provoking Hannah about her barrenness, and this went on for years.

There is a pain that a woman feels that compares to no other pain when she is barren. When she is barren, she is unable to fulfill the purpose of her creation, unable to fulfill the purpose of marriage, and unable to meet societal expectations, which makes her an outcast.

On top of that, Hannah had a rival in her home

who constantly taunted her that she'd had kids for their husband and Hannah didn't. It is inferred in the Bible that this situation often drove Hannah to drink.

> How long will you keep getting drunk?
> Get rid of your wine. (1 Samuel:14 KJV)

These were Eli's words to Hannah as she sat in the house of the Lord, praying with moving lips, yet without sound.

It's funny how we look for anything that can dull our pain, even if for just a little while, instead of turning to God.

Hannah eventually realized that drinking would not solve anything, and she needed to seek God's face, so she caught on to prayer.

Her prayers, however, were not just prayers that asked God to give her a child. No, her prayers went beyond that. She knew that God had made a decision to close her womb because of her husband's favoritism toward her, so her prayers acknowledged Elkanah's prior sin and asked God for forgiveness, and she gave a promise to do better going forward.

We know this because when we ask God for something that we really want, like a house or a car, and we then get those material things, we don't give them back to the giver. We enjoy the gifts provided by the Lord.

But that was not so in Hannah's situation.

Hannah's prayer was for God to change his decision. So she offered everything she had.

- She fasted.
- She wept.
- She prayed till it seemed to others that she was drunk.
- She made a vow to God.

With all she offered to God, she was able to get God to reverse his position on her situation. Hannah offered up her son Samuel, the child for whom she had prayed for many years. It was a vow she made to God, and she honored her vow.

The Bible does not categorically tell us that she had more children after Samuel, but in reading Hannah's prayer in 1 Samuel 2, we see a woman who rejoices in the Lord, with no ounce of bitterness in her; a woman who praises God from the bottom of her heart. Then we read, "She who was barren has borne seven children, but she who has had many sons pine away" (1 Samuel 2:5 KJV).

We don't know how the story ends with regard

to the rivalry between Hannah and Peniniah, but the above phrase may be quite telling.

What made Hannah a praying woman? Hannah was a woman who prayed effectively and knew how to make God change his mind.

As women, mothers, daughters, and wives, let's be in tune with the Holy Spirit and listen for his directions in our lives, that we may pray effective prayers, like Hannah, that could possibly reverse God's position on certain nagging situations in our lives.

25

Forgiveness

───────◆───────

Matthew 18:21–35

Forgiveness—we all struggle with this one from time to time. We know we should forgive one another, and there are several good reasons for doing so, yet we struggle.

Peter brought up this subject with Jesus because it was important for us to know how to deal with our brothers, friends, husbands, sisters, and even parents sinning against us.

We may have heard that not forgiving someone who has hurt us is like drinking poison and expecting the other person to die. This is true, as forgiveness has a way of rotting the insides of the person who refuses to forgive, while the perpetrator of the sin hardly thinks about the sin, yet we struggle with letting go.

When Peter asked Jesus, "Lord, how many times shall I forgive my brother when he sins against me?, up to seven times?" (Matthew 18:21–22 KJV), Peter felt he was doing the brother a favor by forgiving him up to seven times, assigning a set figure to the number of times someone could hurt him and ask to be forgiven. This was Peter's way of self-preservation. "There's only so much I can take of this abuse"—isn't that what we say?

Notice the Lord's response to Peter. He said, "No, not seven times but seventy-seven." It's important to realize, however, that neither seven times nor seventy-seven times are to be taken literally. They are metaphors to denote that we should not come to a point where forgiveness is unattainable. We should continue to forgive, if the person continues to seek genuine forgiveness.

I know it's a struggle. We may think about the constant abuse. We wonder if the apology is genuine or if the person will do something to hurt us again. But if we dig into the text, we will find that the Lord does not have much to say about the brother who is sinning against Peter; he has more to say about the condition of Peter's heart toward the brother. Why is this?

Jesus tells Peter and the disciples a parable about

a man who owed his master a large sum of money. His master was about to have the man's entire family sold to recover his money, but the man begged his master, and the debt was forgiven.

This is who God is. Who can stand before him without debt? He has given us so much, yet we sin against him so cavalierly, without much thought given to how we grieve him. When we do go to his throne of grace and ask forgiveness, the Bible says that he is just and merciful to forgive us.

Imagine if he said to us, "I can only forgive you seven times, and after that, you are on your own." Who can stand against God?

In the parable, the man who had his debt forgiven now had a servant who owed him a small amount of money that he could not pay. The servant begged for mercy but the man, who himself was now debt-free, could not forgive the debt of his servant and had him thrown in jail.

See the condition of the heart of the debt-free man. He was quick to forget that he had been forgiven his own debt by his master and quick to judge his own servant, whom he threw in jail.

The former master who had forgiven him heard about what he had done with his own servant, who owed him so much less than he had owed his master, and the master threw the man in jail as well.

I believe God is telling us that forgiveness is for us and not for the person who committed the sin against us. God wants us to understand his love for his children; while we were still sinners, he gave up his only Son to die for us so that he could cancel the original sin committed by Adam and Eve. And because he offered up Jesus as atonement for our sins, we can walk boldly to his throne of grace and ask for forgiveness as many times as we need to be forgiven.

That love is what God wants us to have for one another—the ability to shake off sin and forgive—so we can have the peace that surpasses all human understanding, which comes from God and ensures that we do not grieve the spirit by not forgiving one another when we ourselves have received the ultimate forgiveness from God.

The Lord's Prayer says, "Forgive us our sins as we forgive those that trespass against us."

And there it is! Now we know the reason why it's there in the Lord's Prayer. It is an important topic because it deals with the condition of our hearts. God looks at the hearts of humankind.

Daughters of the Most High, let us be quick to forgive. *Forgiveness has nothing to do with the person who trespassed against us but more to do with us.*

26

Making Love

Songs of Solomon 4

The act of making love was designed by God. (Have your ears perked up?) The Bible tells us a lot about our coming together as man and wife.

> For this reason a man would leave his father and mother, and hold fast to his wife, and they shall become one flesh. (Genesis 2:24 KJV)

> Be fruitful and multiply. (Genesis 1:28 KJV)

Both sentences above involve sex in the physical realm. There also is a spiritual connection involved, but now, we'll talk about the lovemaking that occurs between married couples.

In many Christian homes, the act of lovemaking is treated purely as an act of procreation—to make more children. It is never discussed, as it is a taboo subject. It is to be seen as a pure act.

It's a pure act in the spiritual realm, as souls are joined together and become interconnected. That is the becoming-one-flesh part.

But the lovemaking—that is purely pleasure. Bringing pleasure to the husband, as well as the husband giving pleasure to the wife.

God created this act so both husband and wife would continue to desire each other throughout the span of the marriage. In fact, the Bible tells the couple not to deny each other this act of lovemaking, except when they are fasting, and they should come together quickly once fasting and prayers are over so that Satan does not tempt either one.

If the act of lovemaking is so important, why do we Christians slap a religious label on it and make it a dutiful act, instead of thoroughly enjoying it as a pleasurable act designed by God for the sustenance of the marriage institution?

Let's delve into the Bible's definition of lovemaking. We can see in the Songs of Solomon that the act of lovemaking is not a five- to seven-minute pounding of the flesh only; it starts with words of affirmation, encouragement, declarations, touching, and enjoying beauty in all its forms—the beauty of the human figure as designed by God.

Foreplay is the lovemaking that culminates in sex as a conclusion.

> How beautiful you are, my darling, oh how beautiful! Your eyes behind the veil are doves. Your hair is like a flock of goats descending from Mount Gilead. Your teeth are like a flock sheep just shorn coming up from the washing. Your lips are like scarlet ribbon. Your mouth is lovely. Your temples behind your veil are like halves of a pomegranate. Your neck is like the tower David built with elegance. On it hangs a thousand shields of warriors. Your two breasts are like two fawns, like twin fawns of a gazelle that browse amongst the lilies. (Songs of Solomon 4:1–5 KJV)

And on and on it goes. What woman doesn't like to hear words like these from her husband? Okay!

Okay! Granted, the animal analogy may seem a bit much today, but remember that animals indicated affluence for people in biblical times.

The point here, however, is to look at how he pays attention to every part of her body, right from the hair on her head. And this is how the lovemaking began, not in bed, necessarily, but perhaps throughout the day—with hidden notes of affirmation or interesting photos in briefcases; with loving text messages; with unexpected beautiful flowers received at work; or unexpected visits at work to drop off lunch; or massages when one is absolutely tired. There are so many ways to start the lovemaking prior to having sex.

It is this foreplay that keeps the marriage interesting—the very act of finding ways to pleasure each other without necessarily touching.

The truth is, the act of lovemaking starts in the brain. This is why Jesus says that if you look at a woman lustfully, you have already committed adultery with her in your heart (Matthew 5:28).

Lovemaking is a soul connection. It is understanding your partner, knowing what makes him or her get in a pleasurable state, and then going completely out of your way to create that pleasurable experience for him or her.

Lovemaking is giving without necessarily

receiving. When the two of you give out of love, then you both receive love. It no longer is just sex, nor is it a duty; it's an act that you both want to experience and fully participate in. Lovemaking is the glue that holds the marriage together. It is not the only thing, in that respect, but it's the one thing that you both have control over to ensure the sanctity of the marriage. Women who suddenly have a "headache" when it's time for lovemaking will slowly chip away at their marriages. Men who only want sex—a slam-bam-thank-you-ma'am—at bedtime will slowly destroy their marriages.

But a slow and steady courting and giving of love throughout the day culminates in a great night of incredible sex, where both husband and wife yield totally to one another.

27

Faith

Genesis 17–18

As Christians, we all talk about the faith of Abraham. The Bible says, "Abraham believed God and it was counted on to him as Righteousness" (Genesis 15:6 KJV).

Most of us know the story of God's covenant with Abraham, making him the father of many nations and promising him a son at the age of one hundred years, when his wife, Sarah, was no longer of child-bearing age.

In reading these chapters in Genesis, I recognized that Abraham was a man very much like us. He did not come with a certain level of built-in belief in God, prior to having years of relationship with him. He faltered in so many ways in his faith, just like we do.

- He told Sarah, his wife, to lie to the pharaoh by saying that she was his sister, instead of his wife, because he feared for his life. He did not say to himself, *I believe in God to keep me safe.*
- He accepted sleeping with Hagar, Sarah's handmaid, so he could have a child of his loins, even though God had promised him a child through Sarah—a covenant child.
- Abraham laughed, just as Sarah did, when God told him of his plans to bless him with a son, Isaac, in his old age.

This faith that we talk about did not come naturally to Abraham or to Sarah. But God chose Abraham and Sarah to be the father and mother of many nations. God was going to use this couple to bring about his own people.

> No longer will you be called Abram. Your name will be Abraham, for I have made you the father of many nations, I will make you very fruitful. I will make nations of you and kings will come from you. I will establish my covenant as an everlasting covenant between me and

>you and your descendants after you for
>generations to come, to be your God
>and the God of your descendants after
>you. (Genesis 17:3–8 KJV)

Notice the number of times in the verses that God uses "I." This was God's plan all along. It had nothing to do with Abraham's belief or faith at that time. God chose him and Sarah. This was God's way of reintroducing himself to a select generation that he would call his own people.

Remember that this was after Noah's flood, when the whole world was wiped out except for Noah's family. Noah had a faith relationship with God, and he built an ark without seeing any sign of rain for years. But after Noah died and many generations had passed between Noah and Abraham, the knowledge of God had diminished, so God needed to reintroduce himself to the world. He chose Abraham, a descendant of Shem (Noah's son).

Again, I wondered why Ishmael, Abraham's first son by Hagar (Sarah's handmaid), was not the covenant child. After all, he was born first, and he did come from Abraham's loins, although the birth of Ishmael was concocted by Sarah and was presented to Abraham, who did not reject the idea. I still wonder why God bestowed the covenant and blessings on Isaac and not Ishmael. God is, after all, *God*, and he is able to make all things work together for good. I now realized that God always has a plan, and he works his own plans and not ours.

As for Abraham's faith, God was working his plan through a flawed man. This made God patient with Abraham as he worked through developing his faith in God. After reading these chapters, I saw a God who repeatedly assured Abraham of his promise to him and to his descendants, in order to convince Abraham that God never changes or fails.

At a point, God led Abraham outside to look at the sky and then told him to count the stars that he saw in the sky. Then he said that if Abraham couldn't count the stars in the sky because they were so numerous, so also would his descendants be too numerous to count. How awesome is that? That God would do anything to convince us of his promise to us. Here again, you see God helping Abraham to build up his faith.

It's hard to believe that an old man of ninety-nine years, with a wife who is not just old, but who had been barren for years, would now give birth to a son. I do understand Abraham's need to be convinced. The whole idea was laughable to both Abraham and

Sarah. With time, however, Abraham's faith grew, and it was credited to him as righteousness.

The truth of the matter is, faith does not just happen overnight. God encourages our faith by taking us through, step by step. It is a faith learning course.

Remember Thomas, one of Jesus's disciples—or Doubting Thomas, as he's commonly known. He was with Jesus throughout his ministry and saw all the miracles Jesus did, including the lives he raised from the dead. But when it came time for Thomas to believe that Jesus had risen from the dead, he flatly refused to believe it unless he saw it with his own eyes. God encouraged his faith by Jesus's coming back for another visit with the disciples, just so that Thomas could see the nail holes in his hands and his side that was pierced by the sword.

When we feel we don't have enough faith, do we just give up and say, "My faith is not strong for this situation"? Or do we go to the Father and say, "Encourage me, oh Lord, for my faith is failing me"?

Be encouraged brothers and sisters, we have a God who understands the frailties of the human mind and wants to help us, in every way, to develop the kind of faith that is not moved by the situations that we encounter in life.

Trust the Lord with all your heart and lean not on your own understanding. In all your ways acknowledge him and he will direct your path.

—Proverbs 3:5–6 (KJV)

28

Love

———————◆———————

What is Love? Have we ever really asked ourselves that question? Is it a feeling or a state of being? Do we choose to love or does the love cupid just strike our heart with it's arrow? Does love grow with time or it just is? Do we have to nurture love, if it grows, or do we just allow it to grow by itself?

These are all questions I have had to ask myself at one point or the other. And I can tell you that I still do not have all the answers to the love questions. Love Is deep.

The one thing I can tell you, is that Love is not an easy thing. It is totally contrary to our state of being. In a world where self aggrandisement, interests, and preservation is the name of the game, the concept of love is totally foreign to us. What we tend to practise at best is a balance. What I mean by balance is reciprocity. If you do this for me, I will reciprocate likewise. If you meet my requirements, then I love you. If you have money or a high earner and your net worth is in the 7 figures or above, then I am crazy in love with you. But that is not love. Love is hard for us. It is such an unnatural thing for us. The closest thing we have to true love is the love of a good mother for her children.

The truth of the matter is Love is sacrificial. You have to die to your natural self and tendencies to find Love. You have to put someone else's needs ahead of yours and then do so without a sense of duty, service or in hope of getting something back in return. Love is not easy.

The Bible defines Love as the greatest between these three, Faith, Hope and Love. If Love is greater than Faith, then Love is up there with God. For the Bible says, without Faith it is impossible to please God. Yet Love is greater than Faith.

So what does the Bible refer to as Love?

!st Corinthians 13 vs 4-8

"Love is patient, Love is kind, it does not envy, it does not boast, it is not proud, it is not rude, it is not self seeking, it is not easily angered. It keeps no record of wrongs. Love does not delight in evil, but rejoices in the

truth. It always protects, always trusts, always hopes, always perseveres. Love never fails."

This is a tall order for most of us. I for one, know that there are a few things I don't so do so well in that list. But in my mind, loving someone, truly loving, has to encompass all the above.

Does Love just happen to us or do we choose to love? When we choose a guy because we have butterflies in our stomach everytime he calls our name, or just because of the way he looks at us, Is that Love?

I believe Love is a verb and not an adjective. I love him or I love her is an adjective to describe your feeling, but Love is an action word. It means you are doing something to show that love. You are being patient, or being kind, or not getting angry (when you should be), or not running through a list of wrongdoings when in an argument. Love is not easy!

So I will say we choose to love. You see, when we choose to love someone, it becomes easier to do the " till death do us part" bit that we all repeat like parrots at the altar.

Why does that make it easier you ask? Well think about it, if you choose to trust your spouse, be patient with him, or her, or you are not angry when he or she has clearly offended you and you still choose to protect your spouse from your family when they want to throw daggers at him or her, that makes for a stronger relationship. And only the devil does not respond to that kind of love.

The bible tells us that nothing else matters more than Love. As Christians, we tend to think how godly we are because we speak in tongues, we prophesy, we have the word of knowledge, we cover our bodies from head to toe, all in an effort to appear holy before God.

But God says none of those things matter as much as Love. Infact, there are only two laws in the bible that God wants us to obey.

- Love God with all your heart and mind
- Love your neighbour as yourself

All other laws are encapsulated by these two laws. This is why Love is very important.

Love is truly an unnatural state for the human mind. I believe we have to go to God the father, and author of Love and ask him to renew our minds, to transform our state of being so that we may learn all the attributes of Love.

What greater love is there when an innocent man is sent to the cross like a lamb to be crucified for sinful men, who do not recognize him as their Lord and Saviour. That is sacrificial love and a great example of true love.

And yet being on a cross he doesn't deserve, prays for the souls of men - the very ones that he came to save. Love is not easy!!!

However, if we choose not to love, who or what are we? As difficult as it may be to achieve true love, we have to keep striving towards it, so that we can lay an example of what the world can be, if we show love towards one another, for God is Love.

God help us in this endeavor. Amen.

29

Fear

---◆---

> For God has not given us the spirit of
> fear, but of power, and love and of a
> sound mind. (2 Timothy 1:7)

Paul, an apostle of Christ, wrote the above statement
to Timothy while Paul was imprisoned in Rome. He
encouraged Timothy with these words, even though
he was jailed for preaching Christ. Why did he do
this? Here was a man who had devoted his later years
totally to Christ and had suffered tremendously for
believing in a Lord and Savior he never had met.

That is quite unusual. Our way in this world is to
avoid suffering as much as possible, even if it is for a
good cause. So why would Paul write to encourage
Timothy, his young protege, to not be afraid but to

be assured that God had given him power, love, and a sound mind?

The simple truth is that it is hard to watch someone suffer for a particular cause and willingly follow in his or her footsteps.

Everything that happened to Paul in his journey was totally contrary to what one would expect of a believer of Christ—or so we may think. Clearly, Paul was not moved by the sufferings that were bestowed on him. Paul had an immovable faith and conviction that made him continue on in his journey.

Paul said,

> Yet I am not ashamed, because I know to whom I have believed, and am convinced that he is able to guard what I have entrusted to him for that day. (2 Timothy 1:12)

When I read this, I learned that it is not what happens around us or to us that destroys us, as we may believe, but what is in us that can bring forth life or destruction to us.

As of this writing, the world is going through a second wave of the COVID-19 pandemic, and there is much suffering. People have lost their jobs, their livelihoods. Some have lost family members and were not able to be by their sides as they passed on. Some have opted for divorces or separation, as the pressure of being locked down with a spouse with whom you no longer have anything in common took hold. Some have become alcoholics or turned to drugs to see them through these terrible times.

But let's cast our eyes away from the pandemic for a minute and look at how the earth is being ravaged by forest fires and hurricanes and how people have lost their homes to such disasters. As if that is not enough, we look at the stock market or our nest eggs for retirement, hoping that might tide us over in the middle of this suffering, but we find the stocks are free-falling like an avalanche.

The above could be enough to make one think of leaving this world, and some have. Suicides are on the rise.

Yes, there is suffering, and everyone is feeling the pinch. Some have made adjustments and are doing well, while some are not doing so well. We probably can agree that the year 2020 came in like a bad wind.

What do we do, as Christians and lovers of the Word of God, when there is suffering all around us? Do we fall away from our beliefs, or are we like Paul, convinced beyond logic that God has a plan for our lives? Do we encourage others who are young in faith, as Paul did with Timothy, remembering that it is not what happens to us that destroys us but what we believe?

It is a difficult time, but ...

Strength is born out of difficulty.

Love is born out of suffering.

Power is born out of weakness.

If we have faith and conviction.

Let's talk about God giving us sound minds. I believe a sound mind is one that stays focused during difficult times; a mind that remains convinced about certain facts of who God is; a mind that does not allow feelings to contradict the Word of God in our lives; a mind that does not allow the events around us to turn our beliefs.

This sound mind is not that easy to attain. As humans, we are spirit, soul, and body. The spirit belongs to God, the body belongs to the earth, from which it was created and will return, but the soul—that is ours. Our feelings, our minds, our senses are all in the soul. We choose what we want to do with our feelings, our minds, our senses. We can choose to believe anything we want in our souls, as that belongs to us.

The mind lives in the soul realm, which is why we need to ask God to help us keep our minds on him.

Ask, and you shall receive. Seek, and you shall find. Knock, and the door will be open. That is what our Bible tells us, but God has already shown us the way forward to a sound mind.

> Do not conform yourselves to this world, but be ye transformed by the renewing of your mind in order that you may prove what is well pleasing and good, the perfect will of God. (Romans 12:2 KJV)

You might ask how we renew our minds, but the foremost question is not *how* but *why*. If our minds are perfect, why does the Bible state that we need to renew them? God knows that our finite human minds can lead us onto the path of destruction. He thereby recommends that we do not conform to what we see happening around us but, instead, that we renew our minds by the reading of his Word daily.

Renewing our minds means constantly delving into his Word, the Bible, and searching God's thoughts on various topics that affect our lives. This is what gives us sound minds.

A sound mind is what will keep us during these perilous times.

Be still, and know that he is God and none other.

Acknowledgments

To God alone be the glory! Great things, he has done!

I would like to say a special thanks to friends and family who have read excerpts of this book at various stages and have offered encouragement all along the way. Thank you!

I also would like to especially thank my son, Mobaderin Akinsanya, who has been my technical instructor and adviser throughout assembling this book. *You are the very best, son!*

Finally, this book could not have been written without our God Most High, who was very patient with me as I asked questions and probed him throughout the process. The words were his, and I was just the vessel he chose to speak with his children, for which I am eternally grateful. Thank you, Holy Spirit, for helping me to be compliant to the end.

May this book touch, transform, and bring solace to the lives of your children. Amen.

Printed in the United States
by Baker & Taylor Publisher Services